The provision of primary experience

Barbara Dockar-Drysdale has a powerful reputation in the field of residential work with deprived children. For many years she has worked in residential homes for children and adolescents. Drawing on that experience, she shows here how the emotional resources of the carer are deployed in such work and how a process of repair may be initiated and strengthened in severely damaged children.

Her approach is based on the ideas of D.W. Winnicott, with whom she worked for seventeen years. In this collection of essays she demonstrates how a psychoanalytic approach can throw light upon, and set examples for, many aspects of work with children and adolescents. In the tradition of Winnicott she combines clarity of thought with exemplary emotional sensitivity. The qualities of tolerance, stamina and perspicacity, characteristic of some of the best psychoanalytic work are amply illustrated. At a time of rapid change in the welfare professions these papers make it clear that the experience of intensive psychotherapuetic work in a residential setting is a resource from which much can be learnt about emotional distress and its management in many other settings.

Barbara Docker-Drysdale is a psychotherapist. She was formerly Director of the Mulberry Bush School and is now Consultant Psychotherapist to the Cotswold Community in Gloucestershire. She is also the author of *Therapy in Child Care* (revised edition forthcoming from Free Association Books).

The Provision of Primary Experience: Winnicottian Work with Children and Adolescents

Barbara Dockar-Drysdale

JASON ARONSON INC.
Northvale, New Jersey
London

10 9 8 7 6 5 4 3 2 1

Library of Congress Cataloging-in-Publication Data

Dockar-Drysdale, Barbara.
    The provision of primary experience: Winnicottian work with
children and adolescents / Barbara Dockar-Drysdale.
       p.   cm.
    Contains revised articles published in various sources.
    Includes bibliographical references.
    Includes index.
    ISBN 0-87668-525-4 (previously ISBN 1-85343-103-6 hb, ISBN 1-85343-102-8 pb)
    1. Child analysis.   2. Adolescent analysis.   3. Winnicott, D.W.
(Donald Woods), 1896-1971.   I. Title.
    [DNLM: 1. Winnicott, D.W. (Donald Woods), 1896-1971.
2. Psychoanalysis — in infancy & childhood — collected works.
3. Psychoanalytic Therapy — in infancy & childhood — collected works.
WS 350.2 D637p]
RJ504.2.D62   1991
155.4 — dc20
DNLM/DLC
for Library of Congress   91-4536

Manufactured in the United States of America. Jason Aronson Inc. offers books and cassettes. For information and catalog write to Jason Aronson Inc., 230 Livingston Street, Northvale, New Jersey 07647.

For John Whitwell and the Cotswold Community

Contents

Foreword

Isabel Menzies Lyth

The first paper in this book, 'My debt to Winnicott', crystallizes the whole thesis of the book, namely the great relevance of Winnicott's ideas to therapeutic work with very disturbed children in institutions.

Mrs Dockar-Drysdale was intensely excited by Winnicott's work and showed a remarkable flair for adapting and applying it to work with disturbed and delinquent children cared for in her own home, in the Mulberry Bush School and in the Cotswold Community. She is well aware of the difference between the psychoanalytic situation with its focus on interpretation, and the child care situation where interpretation may be inappropriate and the child unable to use it. Some of the case histories, therefore, give fascinating accounts of how insight and understanding lead to action to meet the child's needs – action which when successful, helps the child to become more integrated and more communicative. That the work was taxing is very clear: Mrs Dockar-Drysdale does not hide her own doubts and uncertainties; but that it was exciting and rewarding is also clear.

Mrs Dockar-Drysdale was, however, concerned with more than the work directly with the children. This book shows that she was consistently engaged in the search for appropriate conceptualization, both of the children's problems and of the ways of helping them. Winnicott's theories were extended and elaborated in this new situation. It seems to me that she found this necessary both for her own development and for her confidence in her work, and it became even more important when she needed to reach other workers by writing and became involved in trying to help the staff of the Mulberry Bush School and the Cotswold Community to develop their own insights and skills and use them in ways similar to her own. The struggle for conceptualization is very apparent in this book, as is her success in developing concepts and a language which facilitated communication about children and about the work and became a useful educational tool. To some extent the concepts are idiosyncratic and personal, but once one understands what she means by them they are enlightening and contribute much to understanding the children and the work. It is worth making the effort to master them.

The later papers, particularly, are much concerned with the training and support of care staff in the Mulberry Bush School and the Cotswold Community. They show clearly the enormous difficulty of the work and the tremendous stress that staff inevitably experience. Indeed, in Chapter 20, 'Staff consultation in an evolving care system', Mrs Dockar-Drysdale discusses the 'theory of the impossible task', the basic assumption that people, including children, cannot change except in superficial ways. Child care workers themselves may succumb to this theory, indeed often do, although they may continue to 'work with devotion, accept instruction and advice, learn theory and so on'. However, the task is not impossible provided the workers can be helped to confront the task and their own feelings, and appropriate support and teaching are given. The children at the Mulberry Bush School and the Cotswold Community certainly changed, and not only superficially. Mrs Dockar-Drysdale's account of meeting with staff individually and in groups shows how clearly her work with them stayed with their experiences and their work with the children – clinical discussion being of the essence. Theory, even her own conceptualizations, was not used as pseudo-knowledge, or worse as defences against really confronting what was going on. Some of the staff, with her encouragement, undertook personal therapy to further their work as well as for personal reasons.

Partly as a result of her work with them, many of the staff thus developed and matured. The evidence is here in these papers, though rather between the lines. (I am particularly aware of this happening at the Cotswold Community, perhaps because I myself worked as a Consultant there, alongside Mrs Dockar-Drysdale.)

But it is by no means inevitable that the staff of such institutions mature as a result of their membership. I have indeed seen the opposite happen as staff mobilize immature personal and institutional defences against the stresses of their work. The history of approved schools – the forerunners of community children's homes – shows that not only the staff but whole institutions can regress to pathological primitive ways of functioning to the great detriment of the children as well of the staff. My own experience has been that when one tries to help a child care institution to develop better ways of caring for children, there is a significant bonus for staff; if they can go along with the changes in the institution, they themselves also benefit. This happened with the nursery nurses at the Royal National Orthopaedic Hospital as the care system there improved (Menzies Lyth, 1982). It also happened with the nursery nurses in a day nursery when the care system there was changed (Bain and Barnett, 1986). Mrs Dockar-Drysdale does herself less than justice in this respect I think, but she also underemphasizes a telling point about the importance of the careful design of child care institutions – the maturation of the staff being of direct therapeutic benefit to the children (Menzies Lyth, 1985).

There are other 'writings between the lines' that I find myself wishing had perhaps been more explicit. It is not that the message is not there, but only that it is not spelt out and might be missed; though to ask for more may seem churlish when the book is so rich and on the whole so comprehensive. However, a particular point which I found preoccupied me quite a lot in reading the book was the question of management. The most explicit and developed reference to management is in Chapter 2, 'The difference between child care and therapeutic management'. Surely this is a very important distinction. Good child care relying on the principles of hygiene, nutrition and so on, is certainly not enough for these children; much more is needed in the way of insight into their predicament and appropriate action and reaction in relation to it. Indeed, in my experience, there is unlikely even to be good child care in a care situation where the staff are not involved also in good therapeutic management. I have seen children in day nurseries on a cold winter's day, sitting on cold floors, inches of space between their pants and their tops, no one apparently caring. Children are sat up at tables half an hour before the meal; they may sit dressed in outdoor clothes one hour before parents are due to collect them, and so on. This happens in spite of the fact that staff are well aware of the principles of good child care but are not therapeutically involved with the children in a way which mobilizes real contact with their needs.

However, another aspect of management with which I am also concerned has a wider connotation. Winnicott, in considering the role and function of the 'good-enough mother', the importance for the baby of maternal preoccupation, and the symbiosis of mother and baby, makes reference to the setting necessary to facilitate this – the 'good-enough setting', which provides and manages the environment for the mother and baby. Such management ensures that the environment runs smoothly enough, that boundaries are held, disturbing intrusions are prevented or the effects mitigated, and that the mother is free and protected in her maternal preoccupation. Such things include, but are more than, caring and loving support from the baby's father and others; it does really mean that the environment is well managed.

Exactly the same point may be made about the management of institutions which provide therapeutic care for disturbed children: the provision of a setting within which the therapeutic work Mrs Dockar-Drysdale describes can take place is essential. This implies more than just caring support for the staff in their difficult task. It implies concern for the way the whole institution operates, for staff roles and functions other than the directly therapeutic ones, for the maintenance of proper boundaries, the provision of opportunities for the staff to deploy their capacities fully outside as well as inside the directly therapeutic provisions. Such good management is itself therapeutic for children, since it affects the models that staff present to children for identification (Menzies Lyth, 1985). I cannot speak directly of Mrs Dockar-Drysdale's work in her own home or the Mulberry Bush School, although I suspect that her husband provided a great deal of that good management, but I can speak from personal experience of the Cotswold Community where Richard Balbernie's own unusual management ability, his recognition of the importance of firm management and his willingness continuously to review and modify the management situation contributed enormously to the undoubted therapeutic success of the Cotswold Community (Balbernie, 1966). By contrast, in other children's community homes I have seen the best therapeutic intentions and efforts of staff founder time after time because of sloppy management, inadequate boundary control, too loosely defined roles and functions, and inappropriate delegation. Such management diminishes staff, especially as identification models for children; it encourages the development of child and staff subcultures inimical to therapy and provokes delinquency in both staff and children.

What also emerges disturbingly clearly from this book is the tragedy of so many of our children. Mrs Dockar-Drysdale repeatedly and correctly makes the point that the problems encountered in the children that she worked with – mostly adolescents – began in the first years of life, in some basic early failure. One cannot disagree with that view, but supporting it raises very powerful issues. Her work, and that of others of us who work at adolescent level, comes to the problems late, very late. The early damage is too often exacerbated in the intervening years, and the difficulty of the therapeutic task greatly increased. She herself comments on this problem in Chapter 13, 'Secondary deprivation – infant- and primary-school age'. There are other intervening institutions, not only schools, but very importantly, day nurseries, where many of the children who suffer from primary maternal failure, and who later come into community homes, are cared for in the early years of their life. The evidence is that day nurseries may accentuate rather than mitigate the difficulties of these children (Bain and Barnett, 1986; Menzies Lyth, 1989). In other words, it is important that all institutions that care for children be run as effective therapeutic communities. The principles and methods of working described by Mrs Dockar-Drysdale are relevant to many institutions that care for children, besides those of the kind in which she herself actually worked. I hope this book may reach people responsible for some of these other institutions, as well as the audience to which it is more obviously directed. We need to start at the beginning and be there all along the way if more of the tragedies are to be prevented.

It has been a great pleasure to read and think about the collection of papers in this book. They contain a wealth of exciting experience and wisdom and will be of great value to the many workers who are struggling with the institutional care of disturbed children, and who, unfortunately, will have to continue to do so for a very long time to come.

September 1989

Chapter 1

My debt to Winnicott

I first met Donald and Clare Winnicott at a cocktail party in London. We had a rather dull conversation, but just at the end Donald invited me to come one Monday afternoon to Paddington Green, to watch his therapeutic play with children.

I came to Paddington Green on Monday and found Donald playing squiggles with a child – there was quite a large audience. It was not a very interesting session but I had glimpses of what *could* happen and was glad when Donald offered to drive me to the station. We said very little to each other, but enough for me to realize that this was a very remarkable person.

A few weeks later I rang him up to ask him if he would talk to a conference of the AWMC (the Association of Workers for Maladjusted Children). He agreed to come, and arrived, one spring evening, in Warwickshire at the conference.

We had dinner and then, quite suddenly, he asked if I would like to come for a walk with him. It was dark but warm and clear; this was when we came to know each other. We must have walked for an hour or more and we discussed ourselves and our work. Donald had just been very ill – the first time – and his doctor had told him to go slow and be careful. He asked me what I would do in these circumstances and I replied that I would rather be quite dead if I could not be quite alive. He had come to the same conclusion and we went on to talk about all sorts of ideas.

A little later I sent him the manuscript of a paper of mine, 'Frozen children', asking him to read it if he had time. Shortly afterwards he and Clare asked me to lunch with them and we considered the manuscript together. It was then that Donald told me that he was very interested in my work because so many of my ideas were like his own, though I had reached those ideas through my own children, and I had also done a lot of work as a therapeutic adviser to the Mulberry Bush School. This had been set up by my husband and myself, and was the milieu in which I had met 'frozen children', and the phenomenon of therapeutic regression, especially with the kind of deeply deprived children whom Donald described as 'caretaker selves'. I had not in fact read any of Winnicott's writings up to this point, and he was interested to find that I was thinking in terms of 'integration' and 'unintegration' (I shall be discussing these and other syndromes of deprivation later on).

Donald suggested that it could be a good thing for us to talk about our work together, so we started to meet monthly for a whole morning, in his consulting room. These meetings continued for seventeen years; the last one was only a few days before his death. I shall always mourn him.

I had already experienced a personal analysis with a member of the Institute. But our discussions greatly enriched my life and my work, on which he used to make interpretative comments. His remarks were thrown away apparently carelessly, but were tremendously valuable. He used to murmur 'I suppose one could say . . .' or 'I sometimes wonder whether . . .'.

Talking about fame he said, 'when your work is quoted ten years after your death, by someone who does not know your name – this is fame'.

He started referring patients to me – children and adolescents, who would live in our own house and receive psychotherapy and primary provision from me. During this period I had a training as a psychotherapist (with the British Association of Psychotherapists) and was supervised during my training by Dr Barbara Woodhead.

Donald supervised the treatment of the patients he referred to me; we talked about them during our monthly meetings and on the telephone. He told me to ring him whenever I needed advice, and he also saw my patients from time to time and discussed their progress with me.

He and Clare came to see us in Oxfordshire on several occasions, including our daughter Sally's wedding. Once Donald came with me to the Mulberry Bush School, which impressed him. I remember sitting with him on a window-seat one summer afternoon and his saying 'It is wonderful to see such disturbed children so calm and quiet'. The children were sitting about on the lawn and under the trees, talking with their 'special people'.

I published two books of papers (Dockar-Drysdale, 1968; 1973 – both to be reprinted by Free Association Books), and Donald wrote a wonderful introduction to the former. He also chaired me when I read a paper at the Royal Society of Medicine, when he said a lot about my work. I stayed several times with Donald and Clare, in London and in Plymouth. They came to know all our own children who loved them.

I could say much more about my personal experiences with them both, but I want to focus on some of the patients whom Donald sent to me, and on his theories, which I was now using all the time. These children lived in our house, a small manor house with some land, which was ideal for our purposes. I had daily therapeutic meetings with them, and my husband managed the household and also looked after the children and made my work possible by skilful management. We had plenty of domestic help, so that the whole scheme was quite practical.

Susan was a deeply disturbed, emotionally deprived child. She belonged to the category which Donald spoke of as 'caretaker selves'. This meant that one part of the self, mainly super-ego, looked after the little real self. People can manage whole lives on this basis, but it is inhibiting and narrow, with breakdown into panic.

Susan was sent to us both by Professor James Anthony in Chicago. There had been a series of traumatic events in her early childhood – she was not yet four years old when she came to us. She had never slept for more than an hour; she tottered along with her hands groping, as though she were in the dark. She had terribly bad panic states and she often behaved as though she was psychotic.

She was, as I have said, a caretaker self, not integrated as a person. Treating such a child (or grown-up) is comparable with getting to know the nannie (super-ego) of a little child and eventually, if the child achieves a regression, getting back to the original failure of maternal love – in Susan's case at the end of a year. The therapist then takes over the care of the little real self from the caretaker, and all this was true in the case of Susan, who is now a very normal adult. During her first three months with us she called all night and I came to her every time she called. I remember my husband asking how long I thought this would go on and my replying 'for years'.

Presently, one midnight, she asked me for a fried egg and a cup of hot chocolate. I cooked this and brought it to her. She instructed me to feed her the egg in small pieces, going round the edge and then inward till we reached the yolk, which she swallowed whole. Then she told me to hold the cup of hot chocolate, so that she could drink it. This was what Winnicott called an adaptation, and I named the whole of this kind of treatment 'the provision of primary experience'.

Then came a night, at the end of her first three months with us, when she suddenly took the spoon from me, pressed it firmly into the middle of the yolk and then ate the egg outwards.

I knew the egg was a breast, but I did *not* feel that interpretation would be appropriate – what was needed was Susan's 'symbolic realization', as described by Sechehaye (1951).

Susan remained deeply regressed for about a year of total dependence upon me. Then, gradually, her hands stopped groping, she walked normally, she slept well and actually said to me, 'You won't need to come any more, I won't call because I know you will come. I am going to sleep.' That was the end of her insomnia. She began to play and she learnt to relate to people in her environment. Her parents came from America to see her and were delighted by the change. What happened to the caretaker?

Donald and I spent a long time conjecturing about this and came to the conclusion that the super-ego nannie part was projected – probably on to rather dogmatic ideas, so that Susan's harsh super-ego was replaced by my more benign super-ego.

She is now a delightful grown-up, who rings us now and then from the States and who sometimes comes to stay with us. It is interesting that there is no primary repression – she has recently talked about the egg, as an early memory.

James was a good-looking boy, fourteen years old. He seemed to be a normal person in every way, but he suffered from frequent attacks of panic (which Winnicott called 'unthinkable anxiety').

This made it impossible for him to stay at his good boarding-school. His parents were devoted to him but unable to help him, so they brought him to Donald, who later sent him to me.

James trusted Donald, but took some time to feel trust with me. He could talk only at night; I sat on the end of his bed and listened to him. Donald was sure that he was depressed in a deeply deprived and primary sense. He told me that things were best when it was the patient who eventually made the interpretation. I accepted this and worked accordingly.

James talked freely and became totally dependent upon me and I was able to reach 'primary maternal preoccupation', as described by Donald, which I had experienced with my own children. In the middle of all this, Christmas came, and James (in bed) wished to go home. I had great misgivings and rang Donald. He assured me that James could go home for a holiday and would return to his regression.

James communicated easily from then on, and my function was simply to do what Donald called 'holding a situation in time'. What emerged was a series of small traumatic events. One such trauma was that, when he was a baby, his mother was holding him in her arms and, due to an unexpected loud noise, was shocked into near panic, in which she clutched the baby, who became part of the panic.

The mother herself told me of this disaster, without realizing the implication. I never told James about this. He told me of many others – all small experiences of acute anxiety, which turned into panic.

Gradually he became aware of the nature of these panics, and I was able – during panic states – to talk to him about their nature. They had their origins in constant objective anxiety which eventually turned into 'unthinkable anxiety'.

I have never been sure to what syndrome of deprivation he belonged, but I thought he was a 'false self' (Winnicott) and eventually reached his real self. The little real self had been in a shell of adaptation and could not be seen. Now he started again – was nearly reborn.

There were many other children referred to me by Donald at the Mulberry Bush and our own home, all of whom were severely deprived in various ways – most of them recovered, a very few failed. When in 1969 Richard Balbernie (a brilliant educational psychologist and psychotherapist was asked to change a punitive approved school into a therapeutic community for delinquent, very disturbed adolescents, he invited me to become one of the consultants. From the first the Cotswold Community was based on Winnicott's theories.

Chapter 2

The difference between child care and therapeutic management

Good child care is not the same as the preoccupation of the ordinary devoted mother, and therapeutic management is again different, although having much in common with maternal primary preoccupation.

It is possible to look after children very well without being emotionally involved – such involvement is often a matter for criticism if in fact it does appear between grown-up and child.

However, I do not believe that therapeutic management can be achieved without considerable involvement – something stronger and perhaps more primitive than empathy.

Where unintegrated children are concerned, there must be involvement – it is necessary to be able to feel that one is in the child's shoes, not merely to be able to understand what the child may be experiencing (empathy). Ordinary good child care is full of concern, and is also full of knowledge of children's needs – but these are the needs of normal integrated youngsters. It may well be impossible for a well-trained child care worker to look after a really deprived boy or girl. Furthermore, I have known quite disturbed grown-ups to be more easily in touch with these unhappy children than is the well-balanced and well-trained adult, providing that the disturbed grown-up has insight into his or her own problems.

Revised version of a paper presented to the New University of Ulster in 1988.

The differences between child care and therapeutic involvement are best seen by comparing the two kinds of work within the framework of everyday life. For example, child care workers know a lot about food and just what children need to keep them well; therapeutic workers in residential work, while they are aiming to provide a balanced diet, are tuned in to the emotional needs of the child where food is under consideration.

What makes therapeutic management a strain is the fact that one never knows how long it will be necessary. In the Cotswold Community, where I work, there are three units for these unintegrated children, where primary provision is made – in contrast to one unit for borderline integrated and one for fragilely integrated children. In all these units we are accustomed to providing special foods as adaptations to needs and to recognizing the symbolic nature of such provision, even though we may not know what the adaptation means.

Now let us look at the procedure for getting children out of bed. I am sure that all child care workers are warm and friendly to the children they are waking. However, it is unlikely that they will use techniques which then will be faithfully employed by other people.

For example, one fifteen-year-old at the Cotswold Community needs to have his forehead sponged with cool water and a little sponge. Another boy of the same age liked to have his hand held, while the waking person talked softly. Furthermore, we are accustomed to children needing a long time to wake up, and we do not hurry them. Indeed there are times when they need to stay in bed, getting up much later. This is especially true when they are in regression, behaving like babies, and needing to be cared for as though they are only a few months old.

I shall now be quoting from my colleague Helen Morgan's notes, which will give a good idea of the nature of therapeutic management.

My first visit tonight brought me to Mark. On the previous day I had made him a baby badger, called Joe B., and Julian had made him a badger set. Mark and I talked about Joe being very young and in need of a lot of 'looking after'. We worked out that he should have milk at night, spend the night safely in the set, and sit in the kitchen during the day, watching what I was doing. Mark said he would need another, bigger badger, some time – probably in a few months, and he would tell me when he was ready. I spoke to Joe for a few minutes, who answered in a high, squeaking voice, that he liked his new home, and wanted me to wake him in the morning.

I then visited Jimmy. He said he was very worried about his seven teddies, as he felt he could not look after them all properly. He asked me if I would take Jack and Football Teddy, both of whom are hard plaster figures. He was left with the five soft teddies; he said he would be able to manage them, as he and Big Ted could do it together. He said he missed his little rabbit that he'd lost during the Christmas break, and asked me to make a new rabbit, exactly the same as the old one, except big. This rabbit could then help Big Ted to look after the others. I tucked Red Ted up in his new bed, and said goodnight.

When I went in to visit Nigel, he was cuddling Winnie – a pink teddy. He told me that Winnie was lonely, and needed a family. He wanted me to make a Mrs Winnie and a little baby Winnie. Nigel then said he needed something special to eat. I agreed, but said that the idea had to be his – that I couldn't just guess. He thought a while and then started talking about being at home when he was five, and he had found a baby bird in the street. The bird had been attacked by a cat, but was still alive. Nigel took it home, and tried to feed it. The bird refused all food and died. 'It was probably the wrong food', he said. He lay very pensive for a few minutes, then said that, when he was five, he loved Farley's Rusks and hot milk. He talked for a while about how his mother used to give him the rusks, and then asked if this could be his special food that I gave him at night, and I agreed. I left, having put Winnie on his special cushion, and said goodnight.

Finally I visited Darren. I read him a story as usual, but as I was about to leave he suddenly said that he really needed the Angel Delight that Trevor used to give him. He said he did not want it in the same way (at night-time), that would be wrong. He suggested having it during his meetings. I pointed out that since Trevor left (to take over another unit) he had not had meetings. He then asked if he could meet me and have his Angel

Delight then. I said I'd have to think about it, tucked him in and went to leave. Darren said, 'Don't forget Panda, he needs a lot of looking after, like me'. So I tucked Panda in his bed, and went.

You will notice that Helen makes much use of symbolic communication. This is usual, as is the presence of transitional objects. It is important to remember that these boys are aged fourteen to sixteen, but nevertheless, despite average intelligence, like to be read fairly tales, and ask for teddy bears or other soft animals to be made for them, usually by the therapist.

A phenomenon which frequently appears is the experience of regression, either localized or total. In these states the boy goes back to babyhood, curls up in bed, talks in a small voice and expects to be fed (a special food of his own choice).

It may well be that in some community homes regression is recognized and receives appropriate treatment, even though regression would sometimes be mistaken for physical illness. But, in general, regressive behaviour arouses anxiety in adults, who cannot imagine recovery from such a state. Really it is necessary for workers to learn the therapeutic principles of managing unintegrated and deprived youngsters.

How then can residential child care workers employ therapeutic management when this is needed over and above child care? First of all, I would insist that good child care must always be available and used in an appropriate way: therapeutic management can then be, as it were, woven in where necessary. Actually I would suppose that all children in residential care are in need of therapy – they are all deprived (in the deepest sense of the word).

I believe that discussion as a staff group of actual problems of management and other questions, coupled with appropriate reading, can lead to insight and thence to therapeutic work. Very often workers *think* the right thoughts, but do not communicate these to children. For example, the worker may feel that a child is very angry with him, and may think about this, but without passing on the thoughts to the child, saying perhaps, 'I think you are very angry with me'. This link makes it possible for the child to be in touch with his feelings. Books I would recommend are *The Magic Years* by Selma Freiburg, *The Maturational Processes and the*

Facilitating Environment by D.W. Winnicott and, by the same author, *The Child, the Family, and the Outside World*. My own collection of papers *Therapy in Child Care* could be useful. *Dibs in Search of Self* by Virginia Axline and *The Piggle* by D.W. Winnicott are both books about treatments, and are excellent. If one can afford the time and the money, some psychoanalytic help is invaluable. It is quite usual at the Cotswold Community for a worker to go once or twice a week to an analyst. Ultimately it will depend on how much you understand yourself if you are to help others.

I believe that the time has passed in which only analysts, psychotherapists and psychologists did therapeutic work with children. There are now so many deprived young people that I feel child care workers should accept some of the responsibility for treating them.

However, there will be a need in this case which has not yet been discussed in this paper. This is the necessity for supervision and consultation. Ideally this would be available from the staff of a Child Guidance Clinic. I would suppose that experienced child care workers, who have read and thought as well as worked, would be able to fulfil this need quite well. The head of a community home may well have 'enough to spare' and consequently be able to supervise work done by less experienced workers. At the Cotswold Community we have several kinds of 'resource' in each unit. One of these resources is therapeutic, which involves being available to workers for advice and discussion about the boys in their care. These therapeutic resource people do excellent work for their particular unit team (each team works with about ten boys).

Two other important factors in therapeutic management are reliability and continuity – of course both are present in good child care but not, I would think, to the extent to which they operate in therapeutic management. For example, a worker going off for a day or a day and a half will make special provision for a child dependent on him – he may leave a short letter or a postcard, a little bag of sweets or a small cake, usually arranging for this to be given to the child at bedtime. He will never promise anything which he cannot be sure to provide; this sort of failure can have disastrous effects on a deprived child.

Often it is possible for another worker to take care of the child in the absence of the main provider: then it will be he or she who gives the letter or the little cake at bedtime. This stand-in will not, however, make provision of his or her own which would cause splitting between the two workers. The child needs to be deeply dependent on *one* person.

At the Cotswold Community a worker who has a child dependent on him in this way meets the child regularly for short periods when the two talk together. The worker keeps notes on what takes place, especially verbal exchanges. These notes can be discussed with the therapeutic resource or the consultant.

The aim of this work is to fill the emotional gaps left by deprivation, usually during the first year of life.

It may be argued that there will not be time in the life of a child care worker to carry out all these therapeutic arrangements. However, it is true to say that in the Cotswold Community, workers do their own cooking for a unit, housework and so on, and they find it quite possible – perhaps because the therapy is so rewarding – to do this other work also.

Finally, I want to draw your attention to the concept of 'the complete experience' which is important for both child care workers and for those who are trying to provide therapeutic management.

Deprived children have had endless incomplete or interrupted emotional experiences. People have come and gone in their lives with little realization of the awfulness of this coming and going for the child.

The ordinary devoted mother sees to it that the experiences which she gives her children are complete – with a beginning, a middle and an end. She does this intuitively – it does not have to be thought out.

People who are trying to meet the needs of deprived children have to be extremely conscious of what they are doing. Some years ago, Mike in the Cotswold Community told me that a boy had become dependent on him. He described the nature of the close relationship and said, 'I shall not be leaving the Cotswold until Peter has worked through his dependency on me'. Mike will be leaving shortly, but he has stayed, as he planned, until Peter needed him no longer. Peter now has memories with which to fill in the 'holes' of his personality.

I have tried, in this paper, to indicate the urgent need for the provision of emotional experience for deprived children.

There are so many children who need this provision that child care workers need to extend their skills to include therapeutic management. The psychiatrists, the psychotherapists and so on cannot meet the enormous demands, while child care workers can learn how to provide emotional experience, without which the deprived child remains an incomplete person.

Chapter 3

Contact, impact and impingement

I am going to find it necessary here to make certain assumptions, for example, of an acceptance of the concept of an unintegrated state of mother–baby within a unity. I am also going to assume that the idea of involvement as distinct from countertransference is a familiar one.

There are other concepts which I shall be taking for granted, for instance, the possibility of a return, in the course of a regression, to a state of unintegration (Winnicott, 1958) and another possibility, the achievement of integration which I have called a 'progression' in the case of certain delinquents whom I think of as 'frozen children'.

It is necessary for me to start by making these statements because the factors I am going to discuss – contact, impact and impingement – are directly related to work I have done myself, my own acceptance of the concepts to which I have referred having been reached through personal experience, realization and conceptualization.

This communication is subjective; I shall be drawing on personal experience as a mother, a therapist and a supporter of other people doing work in a therapeutic school.

I wish, however, to go on from the theoretical standpoint I have reached, rather than make any attempt here to describe my journey so far. Perhaps the clinical material I shall be using will do this for

Paper read to the Association of Child Psychology and Psychiatry, 12 May 1960.

me, as well as the many direct, and indirect, references to Winnicott's *Collected Papers* (1958).

It may be important to add that I shall be talking about the provision of primary experience for pre-neurotic children. I shall be thinking about contact, impact and impingement in relation to mother–baby unity or therapist–child involvement, because there is no time to consider them in relation to a group setting, where, of course, they are equally relevant, nor in relation to an individual person – which, in any case, I think, is something very different and belonging to a much later stage in emotional development than I shall be writing about.

The unintegrated mother–baby unit must be protected by what Freud called 'the barrier against stimuli'. This surely means the protection given by the father and by the whole secure, containing home environment. All being well, in their own good time, the mother and baby will gradually separate out; when this is achieved the baby will be an integrated person, able to do all sorts of wonderful and awful things and to accept responsibility for doing these things. Support and protection will still be needed from the environment, but in quite a different way.

During the unintegrated phase the mother is in an extremely sensitive and vulnerable state: she is undefended, in the sense that for the duration of the unity she has abandoned her own defences and is completely dependent on the barrier already described, which surrounds herself and the part-of-herself which is the baby, until such time as she and the baby are ready to separate out – at which point the baby achieves integration.

The mother who preserves her system of personal defence will be unable to experience a unity, whereas the mother who is herself an unintegrated personality will slip into a unity as easily as a fish into water but will be unable to separate out in a normal way. There is every sort of variation, including the mother who for one reason or another withdraws concern from her baby.

In the same way, there is a very great difference between the integrated therapist who becomes consciously involved with a regressed child and the unintegrated person who for his or her own instinctual satisfaction becomes involved without concern with a child who needs to regress.

There is also the therapist who, consciously or unconsciously afraid of involvement, refuses to recognize or to meet the child's need to regress, and who, while remaining concerned, defends himself against involvement. And there is the person who, having become involved, withdraws concern from the child.

I would say that conscious involvement *with* concern is therapeutic work where primary experience is needed. Involvement without concern is *not* therapeutic but is delinquent merger. Withdrawal of concern from a position of conscious concerned involvement is negative impingement.

Now, whatever the nature of the involvement, we may assume two people contained within a protecting barrier of some kind. Anybody *outside* the involvement who is not actually contributing to the barrier, but who for one reason or another comes into the zone of the operation of the involvement will affect the situation in one of three ways.

1 The outsider may contact the involvement in an entirely superficial way evoking a reciprocal contact.
2 The outsider may make an impact on the involvement evoking a response.
3 The outsider may break in, impinge on the involvement, evoking a reaction.

Here I would like to give very simple everyday examples of such experiences in the life of a mother and boy, going on to compare these with those of a therapist and child.

A knock may come at the hall door when a mother is feeding her baby; it is possible for her, still holding the baby in her arms, to go to the door, accept a parcel from a postman and return to the nursing situation without disturbance to herself or the baby – there will be interruption and inconvenience of course, but *not* disturbance. This will have been *contact* and reciprocal contact.

The hall door may open, and a loved and accustomed voice call 'May I come up?' Neither mother nor baby are troubled by the call, and probably the mother will reply with pleasure, 'Yes'. The outsider will know just how to come into the room, what to do, how to speak to mother and baby. Should the mother not feel that she can tolerate any arrival she will be able to say so; both she and the loved outsider will understand this sort of thing. Here there has been *impact* and response (which may be either positive or negative).

There may be a knock and at the same time the hall door opens, voices speaking loudly to each other . . . ' Expect we'll find them upstairs –', then the sound of feet on the stairs and the outsiders breaking in to the nursing-couple zone, with good wishes and presents and everything that would seem appropriate, but by now the mother is trembling, and the baby stops sucking and starts to cry. This is impingement and reaction to impingement.

I do most of my work in a therapeutic school where it is impossible for me to be alone with a child with whom I am involved without the likelihood of interruption; both the child and myself are well aware of this. Thinking about such interruptions, I have become aware that they are very comparable to those I experienced as a mother with our babies.

Until very recently my room was in the middle of the school. There was a telephone in the room, there were only two steps from my door to the garden and there were two windows. Nevertheless, this devastating state of affairs had therapeutic uses. Children involved with me discovered – and so did I – that we could be interrupted by the telephone, visitors, other children and yet experience at worst only momentary inconvenience – contact in fact. Sometimes somebody would enter who was in empathy with the involvement – this could as easily be another child as a grown-up. We responded to such an impact.

Now and then, however, there would arrive an intruder, who might be an outsider or insider, but whose appearance on the scene at that moment would make it impossible for me to continue my work with the child because I at once felt the involvement threatened and reacted to impingement, my reaction being inevitably communicated to the child.

There is nothing that one can do with that reaction except be conscious of it in context but, however aware one may be, reaction to impingement is dreadful to experience.

Recently a child in a regressed state said to me, 'The reason why you are the only person who has been able to help me is that you are the only one prepared to be terrified with me.' In working with regression, the danger – the threat – is impingement and reaction to impingement (as with a mother and baby). Isn't it this which produces the resistance to involvement? Reaction is a very primary experience which is naturally feared.

I think only an integrated person, involved and aware of involvement, can experience reaction consciously, that is to say, knowing that this is reaction. An unintegrated person may or may not be aware that he or she has reacted, but in context such a person can only react and may know nothing about this afterwards. I have noticed, when it has been possible to discuss this with people working with me, that they often describe the physical aspect of such reaction – a feeling of burning heat or icy cold for example (connected with panic, rage or despair).

Involvement surely implies leaving one's own defences behind, as it were, there to return to, but not to use in a primary situation where they would be inappropriate. There is no longer any space between the child and the therapist – equally there are neither symbols nor interpretations. These are replaced by experience, what Sechehaye (1951) has called 'symbolic realizations'.

For the child, therefore, there is the illusion of one-ness, because he does not meet the defences of the therapist. There is an illusory barrier against stimuli present, as though both therapist and child are within the therapist's defences.

The risk for the therapist is impingement from without. He has so far, as it were, bent his defences such that he is no longer within them, although they are present as a sort of 'Maginot line'.

What the therapist has to show, above all, is that he is prepared to take the same enormous risk which he asks the child to take. Later there must be outside protection to the involvement provided by a supporter (whom I have come to call a catalyst, because the catalyst remains constant while the components of the involvement alter from moment to moment).

So far I have given examples of a spontaneous normal state of unintegration, of conscious planned involvement as a therapeutic technique and of contact, impact and impingement in these two favourable and progressive states.

I have, however, made reference to the unintegrated mother who cannot successfully separate out from her baby and to the person who, because of an unintegrated self, merges with a child, and I would like to say a little more about this type of merger, which is also open to the outside factors I am considering in this paper.

The kind of delinquent children whom I call 'frozen' have an infinite capacity for merger, because in fact they have never integrated; and I can think of nothing more difficult than preventing a merger taking place should such a child set out to seduce an unintegrated adult. There is nothing therapeutic about such a merger; the aim is not towards integration and separating out but merely instinctual enjoyment of the merger which, until exhaustion or saturation point is reached, seems infinite. Such a merger becomes insulated in a most extraordinary and very paranoid way, and in fact neither contact nor impact can affect something so amorphous.

Impingement, however, is represented by necessary interruption or anticipation, by an outsider, of the delinquent techniques employed by people in a state of merger, and reaction to such deliberate impingement is manifest and acted out, rather than latent and contained, and takes the form of overt panic and rage.

It is interesting to compare this state of affairs with that reached much later, when such a 'frozen' child has actually achieved integration and has reached a point from which he can make a regression. The same child who originally merged is now in an involvement with his therapist and becoming regressed and helpless. The involvement will be acutely vulnerable as previously described, but it will be essentially a growing point and will lead to permanent integration with separating out from and dependence as a separate person *on* the therapist. There will be no delinquent mechanisms employed, and therapist and child will be in the sensitive paranoid state one would expect in such circumstances, but capable of experiencing contact and response. Above all the situation will be one leading to progress. There will not be stagnation as in a delinquent merger.

I have been involved in total and also in localized regressions, and I have found it helpful to compare these different experiences. In the case of Nicholas I shall be quoting notes which I wrote just at the time that he was achieving integration: in the case of Marguerite I shall be describing the actual material which she brought to me during a period of localized regression.

I have recently been through an experience with Nicholas, from which we are now both emerging, but I have had a great deal of support in doing so, both from my supervisor and from the very special milieu in which I work. I very much question whether I personally would dare to continue the steady spiral downwards to the abyss of a regression without such skilled support being given to what so closely resembles a unit.

In this connection, considering Nicholas, who had the opportunity for complete and whole-time regression, I notice that, except at the very deepest point (which only lasted a few weeks), Nicholas was able quite spontaneously to keep whole areas of his life functioning quite normally. For example, he continued to make some educational progress although his teacher was aware of the situation and made no demands on him; he also had a daily session with me which involved communication and interpretation – involving discussion of the regression itself, of which he was conscious.

These areas in which the regression did not seem to operate were, I am sure, of considerable value, since through them he kept some stepping-stones in the present. For the rest he was in a state of complete and helpless involvement with me, and so open to impingement were we both, so appallingly vulnerable, that the amount of concentrated effort required to provide sustained and as near as possible perfect adaptation imposed a strain on me that was barely tolerable, and which only my own environment made possible. Subsequently, following the deepest point of the regression, there was a sudden and very dramatic development in which the contained Nicholas became the container Nicholas. This phase which I would suppose to be the first experience of introjection was remarkable for the force with which this tremendous change was made, and the amount of what seemed to be almost physical pain involved.

Nicholas is a child whom Winnicott (1958) would describe as one of those cases where a caretaker self had taken charge of the real self. In this case the caretaker had never been very competent and Nicholas's life until he came to me had been punctuated by severe illnesses. However, he had after a fashion contained his real self – I would suppose that he did this rescue work at just the time when normally he would have introjected the first love object. In handing over the task of caretaking to me, at long last, in the regression, he once again became a whole person (rather than a shell containing a self).

He actually spoke continually and with suffering of his emptiness – an emptiness which perhaps had previously been filled by the caretaker self ? It was extraordinary to hear Nicholas actually describe most vividly the discomfort and actual pain involved in the experience of first containment, i.e. introjection. He is still terribly sensitive, and so am I! However, at least he is becoming aware of the difference between *impact* and *impingement* – I would not suppose that the caretaker self can hope to protect the real self from impingement whereas the containing Nicholas self finds that he can now sustain impact rather than inevitable impingement, although he is still in such an extremely sensitive state.

One form of impingement for Nicholas and myself took the form of demands. Naturally, I myself made no demands on him, nor did his teacher, while my husband and our family, far from making demands, did everything possible to protect both Nicholas and myself. But, of course, there was a breakthrough of demand from time to time.

A direct question to which he had to give an immediate reply would be intolerable to both child and therapist. Somehow I had to pull myself together and reply for us both, in as inconspicuous a way as possible. Frequently someone else in tune with the involvement intervened on our behalf and led the questioner away from Nicholas. An experience such as the impingement of a direct question is, all being well, only momentary. No involvement could tolerate sustained impingement any more than a mother–baby could do so.

Marguerite's chief dread in her involvement with me was a negative impingement. Describing her babyhood experience, she said, 'The wind blew, the bough broke, the cradle fell – why did the mother leave her baby in the cradle on a weak branch? Why didn't she notice the wind rising?' It was therefore to be expected that the fear of negative impingement would loom large in her regression.

Marguerite was having a short session with me almost every day at this point, but was living in the school, whereas Nicholas was living in our own house and could be allowed as total a regression as he needed because it was possible to contain this in the special circumstances.

Marguerite could not be allowed a total regression, well aware though I was that this was really needed. Accordingly, I tried to plan a localized regression, making adaptations to her needs in areas only where this was feasible, and where I could be tolerably sure of maintaining them. I did not say anything about this to Marguerite; she knew and I knew that we must find a way for her to regress. I offered her sessions, which were accepted; apart from this she had to set the pace, and for me it was a question of being sensitive and aware of opportunities she gave me to make adaptations to her needs, being careful not to commit myself to any adaptation which I was not fairly certain I could carry through to the far side of the regression (when failure would be of therapeutic value and in any case inevitable).

The first of such adaptations was a technique evolved by Marguerite in which she sometimes walked like a small shadow behind me through the school, my share being to have one hand behind me ready for her to hold. (Everyone at the Bush is used to this sort of thing, so that other people's surprise was not a problem.)

At first it really did not matter if something or somebody interrupted and one of us had to let go. In the abyss of the regression, however, it was disaster for both of us for this link to be broken, and I had to be very careful how I released myself eventually. (She never disturbed or interrupted me in what I might be doing, but I only had one hand available for matters other than Marguerite once we were linked in this way.)

Later she indicated that she needed me to bath her. I did this once a week, on a Sunday night, for a whole term – other children knew about this and helped to protect the situation in which we had a bathroom to ourselves. It did not disturb Marguerite, however, for people to come in, although the bathing was tremendously important to her – the disaster would have been if I had left her for an instant. (I did not do this.) I could talk to other grown-ups and to children, and she could do so herself – we both experienced reciprocal contact and impact, the threat of impingement appearing when somebody called me to the telephone (on such occasions I refused to go).

In Marguerite's daily sessions with me she recorded a faithful history of the regression as experienced from within the involvement. The history recorded was that of Jane Hook (a pirate's child), a holding-hand-fish and a shaking-hand-fish at the bottom of the sea. In introducing me to the two fish she explained, 'You can go on holding on to the holding-hand-fish, the shaking-hand-fish you say "hello" and "goodbye" to.' In saying this, and subsequently in other comments, she made it clear that the shaking-hand-fish was the superficial kind of contact and counter-contact which she had with me most of the time; whereas the holding-hand-fish represented the impact and response relationship. We had not yet reached involvement. I was an outsider in regard to the caretaker-self 'set-up'. Impingement was represented by an enormous whale and some very alarming sharks at the bottom of the sea. There were many other characters, both friendly and hostile, in the saga which continues to unfold to this day, and which has been taking place in shell houses which the two fish build – one for each fish. The shaking-hand-fish had a square door to its house, but the holding-hand-fish had a curved door, a curve into which Jane could fit.

As the regression went deeper, Marguerite began to let me co-operate in taking care of her 'little real self '. At the bottom of the sea a shrimp turned up – this, of course, only after the holding-hand-fish and the shaking-hand-fish had been found sufficiently reliable to take charge of the shrimp and had tackled the octopus and the sharks. A small extra house was built, and the fish bought a bed for the shrimp which proved too large for the house (that is, I had no idea just how small the real Marguerite was).

Just a little later in treatment there was a very busy week, during which I hardly ever saw Marguerite alone, and had to be away for some of the time. I had warned Marguerite about this as soon as I knew myself, but I was sure that this failure on my part would be disastrous, as indeed it proved to be. I had counted on at least bathing her, as usual, on Sunday night, but an unexpected emergency made even this impossible. Although this was a localized regression, I was deeply involved and thoroughly paranoid in regard to the very real needs that were making it impossible for me to return to the bottom of the sea!

When finally Marguerite came to see me on Monday, however, I was relieved to find that she was apparently her normal self – pleased to see me, accepting the reality of the situation and ready to continue our adventures together. She always started by asking, 'Where have we got to?' And it was important that I should remember this. On this occasion, however, she asked no questions but began to draw the shell houses and their occupants. She told me all sorts of news about Jane and the two fish; she was gay, she was lively and I realized that I was hearing a lot about her outside real life in the school, which was going very well. Suddenly I saw that there was no sign of the shrimp. For some time Marguerite made it quite impossible for me to ask concerning its whereabouts, until at last I wedged in a question, and she replied nonchalantly, 'Oh, *that* little thing, – it's had flu'. I asked anxiously how the patient was progressing, and Marguerite answered indifferently that, as it had been given no food for a week, it was probably dead or dying – the fish had both been away . . . too far away . . . to take care of it. She added that this couldn't be helped, it wasn't their fault. I said nothing in defence of the fish but asked if they might be allowed to visit the ill shrimp now that they were home? Marguerite now showed me a minute bump in the middle of the shrimp's bed which turned out to be the shrimp terribly ill and shrunken to a mere speck on the paper.

Fortunately we were just in time. It turned out that the shrimp could recover only if it ate up the holding-hand-fish – which it did, and our work together went on.

My apparent withdrawal of concern was a negative impingement by the therapist, symbolized by the two fishes, on the involvement. Jane, the caretaker, had by now handed over to the fishes the care of the shrimp (the little real self). Although I had seen Marguerite during the week and had spoken to her, I had not been sufficiently in touch with her inner world for Marguerite to remain in a state of suspended involvement nor had we reached a point where my failure could be valuably used (as a later failure has been used).

All this bottom of the sea material is still employed by her, although we are now reaching synthesis. The symbols, however, are being used very differently. The threat of impingement (as compared with negative impingement) was symbolized in various ways – sharks, and octopus, and so on. Marguerite pointed out that the fishes, Jane and the shrimp would not be able to defend the shell house against such attack – it was necessary to reinforce the shell houses, which we did with strong scallop shells. (The houses are semi-detached.)

Demands and expectations

Further types of impingement can take place in this sort of work when somebody hostile, or unaware, notices an adaptation to a need being made. In order to explain just what I mean I would like to say a word here about demands and expectations.

Working with deeply disturbed children in need of primary experience of one sort or another, it becomes necessary to distinguish between their demands and their needs. Recognition of this distinction requires insight and experience. I have found it convenient to compare adaptation to demands with adaptation to needs.

The presence of expectations implies satisfactory experience; the presence of demands may mean either failed expectations or an actual lack of any real experience. In either event, satisfying experience must be provided by the therapist for a state of expectation to be possible.

One must not adapt to the demands because this will not provide experience, but only produce more demands. Adaptation to meet needs, on the contrary, can provide needed experience in an intermediate area between therapist and child (such as Marguerite and I use at the bottom of the sea). Such special fields of communication provide a practical form of adaptation unlikely to be disturbed, whereas the 'outside' real forms, such as Marguerite's bathing are naturally more risky, though quite possible and well worth while. However, contact, impact and impingement can all take place within the field of such communication.

Nicholas was ill in bed on one occasion, and a doctor (not our own, who was on leave) came to visit him. He chatted with Nicholas in a friendly and reassuring way, and presently strolled straight into Nicholas's inner world entirely by chance. I held my breath as he talked about a wood which sounded exactly like the secret wood inhabited at that time by Nicholas, who however remained quite unmoved, knowing – as he told me afterwards – that the doctor had no idea where he was, and that if we both waited quietly the trespasser would go out on the other side, which was exactly what happened. (I am not sure whether this was contact or bypass.)

Jean, whom I met for the first time a few weeks ago, is part of her depressed mother. Initially I tried to establish something which could be used by the three of us. I had a first interview in which we all played a complicated form of squiggles – this went rather well. Jean-and-her-mother came to see the Bush and almost at once Jean asked for another game of three-handed squiggles. She made her first squiggle into a circle, inside which she drew a primitive sort of chicken breaking through the shell with its beak – this she put between her mother and me.

It seemed to me at the time that the mother might use contact, impact or impingement in regard to this important communication. What she did, in fact, was to say at once, at the same time handing the squiggle to me, 'I think the chicken is really ready to come out of the egg'. Jean responded with an outstretched hand to each of us.

Gillian had an 'inside sweet shop' which was in fact her first storing place for good experiences. On one occasion, unknown to me, she revealed the existence of the sweet shop to another child. I found her in despair – the other child had shrieked in some moment of rage, 'I'll break up your "inside sweet shop" and steal the sweets!' This was impingement, and we had to leave the sweet shop and move elsewhere. (Much later, however, it became possible for Gillian to create another sweet shop.)

There are circumstances in which impingement can come from within the involvement. I would suppose that this would be more likely to turn up in a regression within an analysis, where external impingement would not be likely to take place in context.

The example I am going to give happened with a child in our own house during a session. This particular involvement had, for various reasons, been so well protected that we had been practically undisturbed by any outside factors. A point had suddenly been reached at which Peter needed an attack from without in order that he and I should experience this and survive (he was constantly in dread of 'the final catastrophe'.

Peter, then and there, generated a panic so powerful that it is difficult to describe except to say that it reached me and was experienced by me, with him, in a way which was actually physical, that is to say, impingement and reaction took place, within the involvement.

Insiders – mothers, therapists, whatever they may be – are desperately vulnerable. They are sure, and their certainty is justified, that they are constantly in danger of impingement. They will indeed experience momentary impingement from time to time, even in the most favourable circumstances, and they will react (the form of the reaction depending on their own personalities). Should they have to react too often, or sustain impingement for too long, there is a likelihood that they will react to contact and impact as though it were impingement. It is therefore essential that a mother in a unity and a therapist in an involvement be protected, as far as possible, from outside dangers.

I want to say something very briefly concerning the provision of such protection to an involvement in a school such as our own. We can protect an involvement:

1   by recognizing and stating its reality and importance;
2   by relieving the therapist's guilt in regard to his or her deep primitive pleasure experienced in involvement – a pleasure which is appropriate and necessary;
3   by planning and management, often involving the whole team, to enable the therapist to take time off, to remain sufficiently concerned about other children and so on – in other words helping him, or her, to achieve some sort of emotional economy, which it is difficult for an involved person to do in a total situation;

4   by accepting some degree of special responsibility for the involved child in the absence of the therapist;

5   by warning the therapist of the inevitability of failure in adaptation, and by understanding the deep despondency which the involved therapist is likely to feel in the event of such failure, especially early in treatment;

6   by helping the therapist, at a later date, to allow the failure in adaptation to *be* a failure, where he may feel a need to rush in with reparation, in a way that will not be of use to the child;

7   by recognizing that impingement takes place without warning, so it is what Freud called *Schreck*, rather than *Angst*, which is experienced (*Angst* being a response, *Schreck* a reaction);

8   by realizing when some not so obvious impingement has taken place, stating this, and being concerned for therapist and child;

9   by helping the therapist to tolerate his hate of the child, which is bound to turn up in this sort of work and if denied cause serious setbacks, but which can in fact be used in a valuable way;

10   by being always, when needed, between the involvement and the 'outsider' – discussing the child at the supervising clinic, interviewing parents, doing administrative work, taking responsibility for mistakes and shortcomings, whether these be real or imagined;

11   by being able to tolerate being used from time to time as a reliable hate object by therapists and children;

12   by being available whenever one is needed – be it only for a few minutes – to discuss the involvement with the therapist, the child or both together.

Chapter 4

Therapy and the first year of life

The treatment of deprived adolescents at the Cotswold Community frequently involves us in providing experience which includes regression. Winnicott described this kind of regression as taking the patient back to the point of failure on the part of the mother towards her baby. The patient may by now be a fourteen- or fifteen-year-old, a delinquent hero who certainly does not seem to accept *any* provision from us. The point of failure is nearly always somewhere in the course of the first year, so that it is to this crucial period that the adolescent must return. Richard Balbernie, the head of the Cotswold Community, and I have tried to supply this much needed opportunity. It would seem, however, that nearly all these boys are capable of regression, although we can only sometimes find just what will help them to return into that first year and just which *stage* will be appropriate for them.

In order to assess this it is necessary to understand that the boys with whom we are concerned are unintegrated. All these disturbed boys have had to survive some trauma in the first year of life – the death or departure of the mother, for example. This has meant that, unless someone has been found who could become involved with the baby, he is liable to go through the years with this trauma unresolved. These unintegrated youngsters have never reached *integration as people*. All the boys accepted for the Cotswold

Paper originally given at a conference in the Glenrose Hospital, Edmonton, Canada, marking the 'Year of the Child', at which the author was guest speaker, and first published in *Association of Workers for Maladjusted Children Journal* 8(1), Spring 1980.

Community are deprived in this dreadful way. Normally, integration has been reached at about the end of the first year. If this has not taken place, no boy can achieve integration without the provision of primary experience through symbolic provision, which can be sufficient for them to reach *symbolic* realization (Sechehaye, 1951). They do not remember the trauma intellectually, but they can *remember through feeling*: if, therefore, we can reach the right symbols, it is quite possible in most cases to bring boys through to integration. Kaminer, in 1978, wrote:

> Some of the determinants of regression to the use of a transitional object are related to a prolongation of the symbiotic state in childhood, and to a mother–child relationship in which the mother insinuates herself into the child's awareness and totally controls the process of coping with separation. This is not the total perpetuation of a symbiosis, but a state in which separation and reunion, which occur repeatedly, must be totally controlled because the painful affect of loss and loneliness is unbearable.
>
> This set of circumstances seems related to development of frustration tolerance in later life. It helps us to understand a characteristic type of object relationship and a particular deficiency in the sense of the self and in the state of narcissistic investment of libido. It thus has important bearing on the entire development of the adult ego.

We are accustomed to regressive behaviour, but not to understanding its meaning so that we can provide what is needed. Nevertheless, we have found that if we listen carefully in communication with boys we are likely to find the vital symbols. For example, a very violent adolescent boy became a little dependent and a little aware of his deprivation. This boy, Keith, asked his therapist for a sack of apples. We went to the bursar for help, and presently Keith acquired his adaptation to needs in the shape of a sack of apples, from which he could obtain apples and comfort at any time (the sack was looked after by the grown-up involved with him). He was sailing ahead, becoming thawed and real, when he went home as usual for a holiday. He never returned: his father complained that Keith had changed into a new person, and this was not what he wanted! When last heard of, Keith was taking a lot of drugs. He had been kept at home by his father just when he was most sensitive. We did not know precisely what the apples meant to him, but we realized that they may well have stood for his mother's breast – his real mother, always ready to feed and love him. Need Assessments showed him to be frozen – in other words, a very ill boy with no ego strength and no boundaries. Working on the principle that the ego is made of experience, we had reached depression and dependence with him, which should have been followed by a long period during which he could be safely dependent. The father, himself delinquent and with considerable investment in Keith, could not bear the change in his boy because it would have had a disastrous effect on what was really a delinquent merger between father and son.

Fortunately, we do not often face such hazards. The boy concerned will actually tell us what he needs, which we then provide. In fact, the provision of symbolic experience leads him back to the beginning of life. The experiences we provide are like stepping-stones which lead to regression. A young patient of mine, called Patrick, knew exactly what he needed. With five other youngsters he was living in our house, and it was one of the other boys who came running to fetch me, early one morning, saying that he was sure that Patrick needed me. I came at once to find him curled up, deep in his bed; he said, 'I've scrambled my tooth.' I then saw a gold tooth in a very 'scrambled' state on his little table. He went on: 'Now I can only eat scrambled eggs, and drink milk.' He showed me the gap in his upper teeth, which made it possible for ∙ him to feel a baby again, unable to bite. For two days he stayed in bed, living on milk and scrambled egg, glad to see us and very contented. Soon he felt 'big' again. He turned up for breakfast on the fourth day, making no mention of what had taken place, but handing me the gold tooth and asking me to make an appointment with the dentist. Following this localized regression, he started to grow emotionally, working well at school, being warm and friendly with us. He never in any way referred to the regression.

We do not interpret regression – it is enough for this to *happen* to the child, with our support and care. He is experiencing early symbolization and realization – I am sure not verbally but with deep feelings – such realization being a central core to his inner reality. It is true that most of the regression, big or small, is essentially an illusion; this is also true for the therapist in that he accepts the child's infantile behaviour and briefly takes a maternal role. This situation was fact when the regressing child was *actually* a baby – the mother and baby set-up gives an illusion of one person, rather than of two, as Winnicott said. Only by providing illusory experience can one care for a child through a regression. The therapist will share this illusory experience, but must not at any point of the regression seem critical or punitive (that is to say, super-ego must take a back seat). When regression to the first year is present, there must be the acceptance by the therapist of various roles at different stages of treatment. The most vital strength lies in the therapist's love and reliability: he must be careful not to meet early needs unless he is certain that he can continue to do so.

I have mentioned a few of the difficulties experienced by a therapist 'travelling' through the first year of life. What I do not yet understand is in what part of the first year we can find failed expectations – the failed care. To help us to do this, I have evolved a Need Assessment, which – when carefully written by a group of reliable workers – can give us quite a picture of the child in terms of the first year failure (see Chapter 22). We have used names for the different stages of evolvement towards integration as individual people. For example, a 'frozen' child is one who has no basic trust and is essentially delinquent.

In no way is the regression unbounded. Often workers are afraid that any regression will go on for ever – for the worker as well as for the regressed child. There is no possibility of such a disaster if the regression is properly managed.

Robert Langs, writing of an analyst and a patient, has said something of great importance to workers with deeply deprived children and adolescents. He says, 'The analyst is continuously scrutinizing his own subjective feelings . . . He must be aware of his own tendencies to distort or misperceive his vulnerabilities, blind spots and defensive needs in the analytic relationship' (1978).

Communication
One of the noticeable lacks in the behaviour of a deprived child is his scanty use of verbal communication: there is usually a stream of

expletives on which he relies for most comments and answers, and there is also a stereotyped list of phrases which are typically institutional. One could argue that such comments hold good for most deprived children, but we must also remember the many who are not technically 'deprived' and who have lived with increasing difficulty in their own homes. These children often present the same picture in regard to communication.

In the Mulberry Bush School, we have always appreciated the importance and value of communication, whether symbolic or otherwise. However, on one occasion we realized a disturbing connection existed between delinquent subculture and a low level of communication. There was, at this time, a disquieting split in the staff group – not openly discussed, but deeply felt. The children responded to this unspoken split by setting up a secret delinquent subculture. There has always been very little delinquency in the Mulberry Bush, which I now realize has had to do with the open communication between grown-ups and children. We – the grown-ups – talked about this difficult situation and agreed that the best hope seemed to lie in the opening up of communication in the school. Accordingly we set up what we now always call 'talking groups' of children, each group talking with a member of staff. The aim was to re-establish talking between children and between children and grown-ups. The talking groups exist to this day in the Bush (and they are also firmly established in the Cotswold Community). At the same time, grown-ups opened up their own problems – the new school had just been built and the move was disquieting. Within a few months the split in the staff team had healed and the delinquent subculture had melted away. This subculture was not directly discussed, but many ideas surfaced in a way which made secret communication unnecessary.

Since that time I have begun to notice communication in a way which I had not appreciated earlier, using groups of transitional objects through which the owners were able to talk of matters never freely entered on before.

Recently, a group of six boys (who, as it happened, all possessed teddies) brought their transitional objects to metal work in the forge. They left the teddies in a row on a shelf and collected them when the work in the forge ended. These particular boys have all come to the same 'talking group' with their bears. The boys had great difficulty in all fields of communication, often sitting in stony silence, while Colin their therapist sat silent also, waiting for something to be said. Presently a quite astonishing happening took place: the teddies became a talking group, and, whereas the boys could not communicate, the teddies had plenty of important matters which they could discuss with fluency and feeling. This bears' talking group has survived for several months and shows every sign of an even longer life. The therapist, Colin Handley, found the phenomenon so extraordinary that he had no idea at first how he should make a contribution to the group – or rather to the two groups. In the end, he talked a little with the bears, who seemed to accept him. He did not, alas, actually make notes about the sessions, but was able to convey the feelings of the group's discussions. I should mention that the bears had different voices from those of the boys: the bears in fact talked in high squeaky tones.

This, then, was a group of transitional objects which came together without 'merging'. It would seem from Colin's description that the egos of the boys worked together to form a group nucleus and a means of communicating with each other in a way which would have been impossible for the boys 'as themselves' at that point.

In another situation, a group of puppets with their owners were free to discuss widely and deeply with a therapist. I am sure there are many similar groups which could be used in this very special way. Of course transitional objects are ideally suited to the growth of communication. In my experience, children – from two to eighteen years – talk to their transitional objects, but rather privately and individually. It is important that I should make it clear that (except for the establishment of talking groups and individual 'talks' between child and therapist) no suggestion is made by us to the children in this context. For example, the teddy bear group came into existence entirely through the instigation of the adolescents.

It is fascinating to conjecture as to the origin of this sort of group communication. I am going to make a guess as to its history: I am certain that this phenomenon could not appear except in a residential setting. There are many things which residential treatment cannot achieve, but here is something which should surely be investigated by analysts or psychotherapists. I do not think that these transitional phenomena can occur where there is not considerable ego development. The people whom I have described were unintegrated boys on the way to integration as individuals. These children and adolescents are beginning to function in terms of a fragile ego. Is it possible, do you suppose, for such a group to project the ego nucleus on which the group is based, in such a way that the nucleus functions and communicates in a manner that the individual member of the group cannot achieve? A fascinating book (Grolnick, 1978), recently published in the United States, on transitional objects and transitional phenomena gives wonderful descriptions of many transitional objects and their history. There is nothing concerning 'groups' of transitional objects. I would suppose that this sort of 'group' could only turn up in a residential setting – this is certainly the first time I have seen such an astonishing development.

Turning from groups to individuals, one can find a wealth of information concerning the child and the transitional object (the first 'not me' possession). Michael, aged three, had two objects – Giggle and More-Giggle. These were rather shabby golliwogs which went everywhere with him. Giggle was 'good' and More-Giggle was 'bad' and constantly punished. Ultimately, Michael threw More-Giggle out of a train window, leaving himself with the 'good' Giggle. This was one of the few times when I have witnessed the end of a transitional object. Usually they fade away, ceasing to be important – they lose their 'life'. It is interesting that, in the Cotswold Community (where I work as a consultant), it is quite usual for a worker to say that a transitional object is 'very much alive', meaning of course the high degree of investment shown by the child in the object.

The possibility of communicating with a child through his transitional object has been explored. The transitional object or group of objects may speak on behalf of their owners, in a way which brings the therapist to realization concerning the children. Frequently there is a shared responsibility for the transitional object between the owner and the therapist. This arises easily and naturally, because the therapist helps in the caring for the transitional object. For example, a little bed may be made, a tiny cup of orange juice provided for the transitional object and many other needs may be met by direction of the owner. I assume that these needs are also what the child requires, if symbolic communication is carefully used. The danger is, of course, that the worker may inadvertently initiate the further meeting of needs because of his own interest and enthusiasm: such contributions, however, are unlikely to benefit the child. I quote from Robert Langs's *The Therapeutic Interaction: A Synthesis*:

> Because of the differences in his role and functions, we need a different classification of the communicative properties of the analyst. This study may be initiated by identifying the source of his most frequent interventions: silences, confrontations, questions, interpretations, and reconstructions. We may consider next the extent to which he offers valid interventions, the qualities of his management of the framework, and frequency and nature of his errors. The analyst's erroneous interventions may primarily communicate his own pathological intrapsychic fantasies and introjects, and be largely verbal-fantasy communications. (Langs, 1977)

Most children have a transitional object at a certain stage of their early development, but deprived children in treatment seem to discover a transitional object for the first time.

It is of course an easier task for the therapist if he is dealing with a group of transitional objects. They will give clues in the course of their discussion, which will throw light on their meaning. However, symbolic communication between a child and a therapist is a way in which we can build up communication as we gradually come to understand the child's symbols. It is very rewarding to communicate in this way, and it will soon become clear what the symbols represent. There is a temptation to interpret at this juncture, and it is important to realize that once interpreted – however correctly – the symbols will be abandoned, so that, unless one is sure that the child is very near an understanding of his communication, it will bring an end to the slowly growing insight of both therapist and child. I once worked with a child aged nine, for nearly two years, during which we discussed his 'castle' in minute detail. I remember that when he decided to let me into his 'castle' it was as a plumber in a small van that I was allowed to cross the drawbridge, with instructions to do something about the out-of-date plumbing.

There are innumerable examples of transitional objects and transitional experience. Symbolic communication is the vehicle which carries the early experience for the child. Winnicott (1958) wrote:

> It is not difficult to see that in the case of every infant at least these three things have to happen:
> 1 The infant has to make contact with reality.
> 2 The personality of the infant has to become integrated, and the integration has to gain stability.
> 3 The infant has to come to feel he lives in what we see so easily as the body of that infant, but which at first we know is not felt by the infant to be significant in the special way we know it is.
>
> Three things: reality contact, integration, sense of body.

Delinquent adolescents and transitional objects

Winnicott realized, conceptualized and communicated the phenomenon of the 'transitional object', which he described as 'the first not me possession'. Briefly, the transitional object belongs to that stage in a baby's evolvement when he is beginning to separate out from his mother. You will remember that the primary unity consists of the mother and baby being part of each other. One would think of this important process taking place near the end of the first year of life. The transitional object bridges the gap between mother and child – this is an illusory bridge, but nevertheless the transitional object itself is real.

I am describing this phenomenon taking place not between a mother and baby, but between therapists and delinquent boys of fourteen years and older in the Cotswold Community. This is especially interesting because the transitional objects in the Community turn up in exactly the circumstances of a baby separating out from the mother. Since these delinquents can usually communicate at this stage, in a way which makes it possible to understand the nature of this important experience, we can learn much about the evolvement of the transitional object.

Kaminer in 1978 wrote: 'Some of the determinants of regression to the use of a transitional object are related to a prolongation of the symbiotic state in childhood.'

We are accustomed in the Community to the task of bringing unintegrated adolescents through regression to integration, and so on to secondary experience. At some point in this process it is usual for a boy to ask for a transitional object. We do not mention the object, nor do we suggest possible objects as suitable for this particular boy, who will in fact name the object quite clearly, usually to his therapist. Teddy bears made by the 'special person' are much in demand; recently a boy demanded a badger, which was duly created; and a little cushion and a very old pair of socks are a few of the many transitional objects which have been appearing in the Community. Usually the object is cared for, 'living' in the boy's bed for the most part. It is never actually destroyed, though it may be ill-used and damaged from time to time. Such an object was a 'potato man'.

It seems frequent that the transitional object is a stepping-stone to regression, and that the boy is already deeply involved with a special person. In such cases the object is helping to fill the gap between boy and therapist, but whereas transitional objects usually turn up to bridge the space between mother and baby, in the course of separating out, here in the Community the transitional object is first needed when there is a measure of dependence between boy and therapist – on the way into and out of regression. Following regression, the object may be treasured or handed over to the therapist for special care: sometimes a particular kind of food is needed at a regular time for weeks on end. On the other hand, the object may gradually fade out, losing its importance and finally completing its life at the bottom of a cupboard.

I cannot communicate the astonishing situation in which a sixteen-year-old who is delinquent, violent and (so far) unable to make relationships can play with and care for his transitional object. The therapist may need to make some clothing for it, and frequently provides a little cup and other suitable provisions at the request of the boy. Never must the transitional object be washed (the smell is always important) but the slightest hole needs to be mended at once by the therapist.

One boy kept an old pair of socks as a transitional object. Dennis treasured these socks and wore them now and then. They had been mended so often that they seemed to be made of lace. Jo (at the Cotswold Hostel in Oxford) brought me the pair of socks and explained that she realized how valuable they must be to Dennis, but that they would soon be just holes if they continued to be worn at all. Jo and I discussed the problem and decided together that we could make a little person out of the two socks, which we hoped could then survive as long as Dennis needed it. We realized that we were taking a great risk – Dennis might be enraged or despairing as the result of our action. Nevertheless it *felt* right to both of us. Jo made the little person and presented 'him' to Dennis when he returned from a weekend visit to his home. Dennis was, to our great relief, delighted: he fairly beamed with pleasure, asking only 'You did use both socks?', and when Jo assured him on this point he collected the little person (who never had a name) and settled him on his mantelpiece. When, months later, he was ready to go out to work, he asked Jo to make overalls for the little person, who would also start work. Ultimately, when Dennis actually left the hostel, he took the little knitted person with him into the outer world.

One of the most dangerous disasters which can befall the transitional object is for the therapist to leave the Community *before* the boy has worked through the experience with a transitional object, which no longer 'lives' despite the efforts of the boy to prolong its existence. There is also the more frequent problem where the boy needs to progress to another more integrated unit, usually accompanied by his transitional object, which can no longer be used. The bridging of the area between a boy and his therapist cannot usually be transferred to another person. When a therapist leaves the unit when a boy is still at the transitional phase, it is common for another therapist to take over the task of responding and providing for the boy, using the original transitional object as a bridging factor. Such an attempt is doomed to failure. It is my impression that the transitional object arrives on the scene towards the end of a regression, when the boy is coming to a borderline integration. This borderline stage is like a watershed, where the recovering boy is balanced, sometimes pushing on to integration, at other times falling back to a state of unintegration. The transitional object appears to accompany the boy as he rocks on the watershed, sometimes seeming to be a helpless little animal, at other times travelling forward in an attempt to ensure firm integration.

I believe that the transitional object provides an ego force; and just as the baby seldom uses the transitional object in a negative way, so the adolescent delinquent seems to regard the transitional object as a reliable ally which he uses well. However, there are times when the transitional object is seen as something 'bad', on which many of the boy's angry feelings are projected: I have already mentioned the little boy who owned two identical golliwogs, one of whom was felt to be 'good' and the other 'bad'.

I am quite sure that there are many transitional objects in every community home, but I wonder if they are treated with due respect? Are they recognized for what they are? It would be easy to be critical of a fifteen-year-old boy who takes his transitional object to bed with him. Often we have to advise boys to leave their transitional objects in our care while they go home for a holiday. There have previously been unhappy experiences with parents or foster parents who may be unable to tolerate the presence of the transitional objects.

It would be easy for anyone to react in this sort of way unless they had learnt about the importance of a transitional object in the boy's life. Parents, especially, are alarmed by what to them is merely regressive behaviour. Workers often worry also in case the boy with a transitional object will be teased: actually other boys in a residential place rarely tease in this context. New boys, on the other hand, are both envious and angry – until they have a transitional object of their own.

One must be prepared, if one is doing therapeutic work, to respect the transitional object itself, so that we can communicate with the transitional object while it may still be impossible for the young owner to allow or reply to our communication directly (as in the group of teddy bears).

Winnicott, writing about primitive emotional development, said:

> The infant comes to the breast when excited, and ready to hallucinate something fit to be attached. At that moment the actual nipple appears, and he is able to feel that it was that nipple that he hallucinated. So his ideas are enriched by actual details . . . The mother has to go on giving the infant this type of experience. (Winnicott, 1958, pp 152–3)

The use of a transitional object has much in common with the baby at the breast.

I have tried, in this paper, to bring together therapeutic regression and the first year of life. To do this I have considered three factors: regression, symbolic communication and transitional objects.

I wish to end by quoting from Alfred Lord Tennyson.

> The baby new to earth and sky,
> What time his tender palm is prest
> Against the circle of the breast,
> Has never thought that 'this is I:'
>
> But as he grows he gathers much,
> And learns the use of 'I', and 'me',
> And finds 'I am not what I see,
> And other than the things I touch.'
>
> So rounds he to a separate mind
> From whence clear memory may begin,
> As thro' the frame that binds him in
> His isolation grows defined.

Chapter 5

About integration

I think that it is a fallacy to suppose that children who have been emotionally deprived, but who have achieved borderline integration as whole people and who are physically adolescent, should also be *emotionally* adolescent. We have always supposed that borderline integrated children should have secondary experiences, which implies an adolescent culture. In fact, in the course of normal development, children are integrated – more or less – at the age of a year. Those who are deprived and who have failed to integrate regress in the course of treatment to *the point of failure* (Winnicott). This may be at any stage of early development. Children *know* the point to which they need to return, just as they *know* what they need as symbolic adaptations.

The failure (of maternal provision) will be in the course of the first years and is fixed like a fly in amber in the unconscious memory. Once we have met the boys' needs and they begin to evolve, this may be from any stage of development. At the moment we have a gap between primary and secondary provision, and this gap must be bridged.

We see some evidence in the Cotswold Community that this is happening after a fashion, but not with appropriate support. Winnicott has pointed out that integration is followed by a paranoid phase (something like Klein's paranoid schizoid position in which the child defends his newly established personality, which must be very fragile.

We have seen this paranoid phase in borderline integrated groups without understanding the implications. If we accept the idea that integration can take place at many different points, we must face the fact that we are not treating a coherent group of integrated adolescents, but a collection of children at different stages, who may have many varied needs – including regression and transitional experiences of every kind.

There have been successful regressions which have turned up in our borderline integrated groups from time to time. However, the present culture among the children in Northstead* ignores the need for transitional objects, which are condemned as 'babyish' (whereas of late in Larkrise such objects have been accepted by the boys). There is a gulf between the Cottage primary experience and the Northstead culture, where children actually repress their memories of the Cottage experience because of the attitude of their peers, to which they feel they must adjust. I have thought that this is Freud's primary repression of earliest experiences, but I do not think now that this idea is valid. The boys in Northstead do eventually ask to visit the Cottage and remember their early experiences. Every effort is made to preserve contacts with the Cottage or Springfield, but for a long time the boys make it plain that they have now left all this behind and conform to the peer group. They are frequently delinquent, hard and paranoid in their attempts to conform to the requirements of the peer culture and the results are chaotic.

Actually, we are working here with a mixed group at different stages of development, who need to be considered in terms of their individual needs. The delinquent aspect, for example, is a falling back on self-provision, in the absence of therapeutic provision.

I am not attempting to indicate what needs to be the therapeutic approach to these difficult problems, I am only trying to suggest the nature of the problems. We know that children do not need to reach complete integration with us. There is every indication that they continue in the main to evolve after they leave us, to achieve more or less complete integration in the course of their lives. What I am suggesting is only a development of this idea.

To take an example. A boy at a paranoid stage needs a great deal

---

* Northstead, Larkrise, Springfield and the Cottage are four of the households of the Cotswold Community. Northstead and Larkrise are where the more integrated boys live and work, whereas Springfield and the Cottage are for the unintegrated.

of empathy, because it is natural that he should defend his fragile self. A boy at Larkrise went into complete regression as a sheep. This lasted only a brief time and he then continued to evolve very well.

Peter Millar (head of education in the Cotswold Community), who has been reading round these problems, suggests that we have not sufficiently considered the significance of the latency period – lying between primary and secondary experience and seen originally as a sort of lull following the experience of the Oedipus complex. However, it now seems that the latency period is very dynamic and important. The essential factor during the latency period is identification, the sort of identification of the small boy who gardens *with* his father. This would suggest that there should be a period when adults supply the kind of adventurous enterprises with which the boy can *identify*. This means the grown-ups having and providing adventurous enterprises with which the boy can identify and become involved. This seems to me to be important in all fields – whatever the grown-up can offer.

Thus the boys can reach secondary experiences. This clearly applies only to those boys who integrate around the latency period. Obviously all boys must be carefully assessed shortly after reaching borderline integration.

Chapter 6

Reality

I shall be presenting a highly personal point of view in regard to reality, rather than attempting a survey of other people's thoughts on the matter. This does not mean that I am 'right' or 'wrong', but certainly I shall be speaking with conviction from the particular position which I have reached at this point.

There are two kinds of reality. One is outer, which is individual in that each of us perceives outer reality in a different way – for example, the people and the objects in a room. The other is inner reality, which is unique for each of us: it is furnished from our earliest experiences onwards – experiences symbolized, realized and arranged within us as the order of our inner worlds.

As babies, we had neither outer nor inner reality, existing as we did in a Golden Age – a state of illusion. Babies thrive on this illusion, so that, although born, they continue to feel part of their mothers, just as their mothers feel part of them (should outer reality impinge on this illusory perfection, it will be felt as trauma). Winnicott has described how babies create their mothers and how mothers are there to meet creation by their babies – this is all an essential illusion. Only as the baby obtains enough primary experiences from his mother – her breast, her arms, her smile – can any baby change slowly from being contained by the mother to being himself a container of inner reality. This great change can take place only if enough transitional experience is available – bridging the gap between the mother and the baby, so that

Written in 1973 and first published in the *Journal of Educational Therapy* 2(2): 1–17, 1988.

eventually the baby can tolerate becoming an individual in his own right. Initially, however, all babies *must have been contained* – indeed, those who have never had this illusory 'part-of' experience become static, living in a limbo, neither contained nor containing, with neither outer nor inner reality clearly defined. Those who have been prematurely disillusioned (having had *something* however inadequate) by separation, either emotional or physical, will become the wild ones, who are always endeavouring to mould reality into something with which to merge – that lost illusory mother.

A child's view of outer reality will depend upon his inner world. Should this be peopled by tormenting devils and raging monsters, then outer reality will be a threatening and terrible place: the baby who has been constantly deprived and frustrated is full of helpless rage (the devils and monsters) which one day may be seen as panic, violence, murder and destruction. Only the infant who has had 'good-enough' early experience can gradually, in the course of the first year, become a person, reaching the realization that his mother is another, separate person from himself in outer reality. By then, however, he has incorporated her symbolically into his inner world, and is ready to be disillusioned through her external failure to make perfect adaptations to his needs – *providing that* this failure happens very gradually, so that slowly the Golden Age is forgotten (that mechanism which Freud called 'primary repression' takes place) and the baby comes to love and hate his mother as a real living person in the world. Artists, poets and musicians have not repressed these earliest experiences – *they* can recall for us what we have never thought about because it was before thought.

> Turn wheresoe'er I may,
> by night or day,
> The things which I have seen I now can see no more.
> (Wordsworth, 'Ode on the Intimations of Immortality')

You may have read Winnicott's description of the first year of life, and the discovery of reality. He wrote:

We can now say why we think the baby's mother is the most suitable person for the care of that baby; it is she who can reach this special state of primary maternal preoccupation without being ill. But an adoptive mother, or any woman who can be ill in the sense of 'primary maternal preoccupation', may be in a position to adapt well enough, on account of having some capacity for identification with the baby.

According to this thesis a good-enough environmental provision in the earliest phase enables the infant to begin to exist, to have experience, to build a personal ego, to ride instincts, and to meet with all the difficulties inherent in life. All this feels real to the infant who becomes able to have a self that can eventually even afford to sacrifice spontaneity, even to die.

On the other hand, without the good-enough environmental provision, this self that can afford to die never develops. The feeling of reality is absent and if there is not too much chaos the ultimate feeling is of futility. The inherent difficulties of life cannot be reached, let alone the satisfactions. If there is not chaos, there appears a false self that hides the true self, that complies with demands, that reacts to stimuli, that rids itself of instinctual experiences by having them, but that is only playing for time. (Winnicott, 1958, pp. 304–5)

The baby discovers reality in all kinds of ways, but essentially through his mother: he smiles at her and learns about his smile because he sees it reflected in her face. He discovers depth and dimension in his little landscape through touching from his mother's arms what he has perceived (many deprived children only perceive in two dimensions). He discovers time – his own biological time – through the rhythm of feeding and care which he and his mother have established (I know deprived children who can read the time on a clock face but who have no sense of 'real' time within themselves). His discoveries are innumerable and his explorations boundless: his mother is the ship on which he makes his voyages. Reality is there to be tested: gradually he will make his own way, but not too soon.

Suppose, for example, that a two-year-old came to the top of a staircase, which from his eye-level would appear to be a smooth, sheer slope – he would withdraw in fright, and could have a hidden unknown fear of a staircase buried within him for years to come, although ultimately he would climb up and down stairs. He would need to have made this discovery with his mother initially, sitting beside her, bumping gently down from step to step, discovering reality without shock.

Providing that he has had this good-enough experience he can stand the painful realities, both the outer and the inner kind, learn to tolerate frustration, to contain his anger and his hate, anxiety and envy, as well as his love and trust. In the same way, he can stand bumps and cuts and bruises – all the minor hurts of early childhood, if his mother is there to comfort him. A stomach-ache can cease being felt as persecution.

He begins to make reparation in respect of harm he feels he has done to those he loves (especially his mother) in inner and outer reality – he will pat his mother's foot gently if he has bumped into her, try to put things straight, to clean up, to smooth. His intent look will show how real and deep are his feelings towards restitution for damage which may have been done only in terms of inner reality. All this, and yet he is still a toddler – but the children I meet in my work have often not now reached (however old they may be) the achievements of such a baby. What does 'reality' mean to them? They say:

> *Really* you know, all husbands and wives hit each other.
> *Really*, mothers don't want babies – they have them by mistake.
> *Really* living – what you call living – is just a long way of dying.
> *Really* I was dropped on some stony ground from an aeroplane – that's how I was born. My mother found me by luck.
> *Really*, you don't understand – I've murdered love.

What has happened to their perception of outer and inner reality? How can we change this perception? Only, it would seem, by going back to the point of failure in their mother's provision, by providing new first experience with which to fill an inner reality, a basis from which outer reality can be seen afresh.

So far I have said nothing concerning fantasy. Winnicott says:

> It will be seen that fantasy is not something the individual creates to deal with external reality's frustrations. This is only true of fantasying. Fantasy is more primary than reality, and the

enrichment of fantasy with the world's riches depends on the experience of illusion. It is interesting to examine the individual's relation to the objects in the self-created world of fantasy. In fact there are all grades of development and sophistication in this self-created world according to the amount of illusion that has been experienced, and so according to how much the self-created world has been unable or able to use perceived external world objects as material. (Winnicott, 1958, p. 153)

Fantasy of the deepest sort is unconscious and difficult to reach, and a forerunner of inner reality. Fantasying is the superficial imagining which one meets so often among deprived children where it is usually concerned with the manipulating of intolerable and frustrating objective reality, whereas fantasy belongs to the roots of inner reality and earliest experience.

There are, however, all kinds of conscious fantasying which enrich the life of normal children, providing them with material from which to tell fairy tales, to invent play and to make good use of story-tellers and games. Creativity comes from a deeper source – from the 'stuff which dreams are made on' and is always symbolization of realized emotional experience. Play comes into this vast area of transitional experience: ideally, a five-year-old (in contrast to a baby) is neither omnipotent nor helpless, neither able omnipotently to control his mother any more nor at the mercy of his own violent instincts. Play helps him to come to terms with terror and violence, and to strengthen the boundaries of himself.

Recently I have been playing over a short period of time with a small boy, Roger, who is recovering slowly from a state of autism. Roger had never been able to separate out from the primary unit with his mother. I am going to talk a little about his play and his communication, because he opened the door of his inner world and revealed its reality.

In the first week, I had a session with Roger in the bathroom opposite my room, where there is a loo. We used the loo as play material, pulling the chain, floating paper boats and discussing the various plumbing equipment. Roger was anxious but excited, and when I said that very little boys could be afraid of going down the loo when the chain was pulled, he replied 'But *I* didn't, did I?' He spoke of being frightened of the noise when the chain was pulled, but asked me to pull it and held tightly to my hand while he peeped over the edge (we sat on the floor, so as to make his height that of a toddler). I said how upsetting it would be to a little boy for what he did in the pot – this valuable stuff from inside him, which he offered to his mother – to be put down the lavatory without praise and appreciation. Roger said nothing to this, but looked very pleased with me, and did not, for once, say 'Silly Mrs Dockar-Drysdale!'

In the second week, he came to see me and drew a rainbow. I asked, 'What do you find at the end of a rainbow?' He replied at once, 'A pot'. He asked me to draw him a pot (at the end of his rainbow), which I did, making it a baby's potty. He asked me to draw him, as a baby, sitting on it. I did so, and asked, 'What is in the pot?' He answered, 'Gold, of course!' Later, when I went to Jenny (in charge of crafts), I asked her if she would let Roger make a pot with her (explaining my reasons). I said that I'd provide 'gold' in the form of chocolates wrapped in gold paper (to represent gold equalling faeces). I then talked with Brigitte and we agreed that Roger could bring the pot to her and that she could then accept it from him and one would hope that he would experience symbolic realization.

All this was carried out. Roger was eager to make the pot, which he took some time over, and which had to be painted (brown) and fired. Then he put the 'gold' in it and presented it to Brigitte one day at a staff meal. He was apparently full of joy, and cried, 'Now you'll be rich – I've given you all this treasure, you can get everything you want!', or words to that effect.

Since this event there has been considerable change in him: he is looking rosy and well, moves more freely and communicates in a more coherent way. He has been seen to go into a lavatory and to pull the chain. There is some disagreement about whether or not he is soiling, but it seems that most of the time his pants are only smeared. In any event, he has had quite an important experience, brought about by a group of people working closely together to ensure its completion.

The following week he came to see me and told me about the pot of gold and his presentation to Brigitte and her gratitude and pleasure. He then asked me to draw Brigitte and Mr Roger himself giving her the pot of gold. I did my best and he shrieked with pleasure.

Later, Roger came for a session. He drew me and then asked me to draw a picture of 'Mr Roger sitting on his potty'. We then played squiggles and I drew Mr Roger sitting on an elephant (the trunk equalling drainpipes, etc.). Roger then made a *snake*. I then made a cat with a *tail*. At this point, things started to happen. Roger asked me to draw a loo, and 'Little Mr Roger sitting on it'. I did this; at once he went into action, pulled the chain in the drawing and asked me to draw Mr Roger *down the loo*. He then ordered a pipe and a further picture of Mr Roger, turned over the paper and drew the 'shit baby' Roger going down the drain, writing in large letters 'sharp bends'. He went on to another sheet and said, or rather cried, 'He's come to the waterfall marked "danger".' He then drew, beyond the waterfall, Mr Roger in 'The Lake'. Above this he wrote 'trapped'. There was tremendous feeling communicated in all this.

On a later occasion, he asked me to draw Mr Roger going for a walk. Then he took over and drew a bridge. His first Mr Roger was quite like mine, but soon this Mr Roger was again a 'shit baby'. He crossed the bridge, turned over the page, and then Mr Roger went up a hill, at the top of which was a *well*, exactly like a loo seat. He then drew Mr Roger coming down the hill, but suddenly sent him up again. I had to draw the hill – and make him fall *down the well*, again trapped at the bottom; but he wrote, 'Mr Roger *thought* he was trapped.' I said firmly, 'But there *is* a way out', and drew a passage on the other side, to his order. He then turned over and wrote, 'Then he found a secret passage out of the hill' (out of his mouth), drew the passage and put arrows to show Mr Roger the way. He exclaimed, 'He has tried lots of passages which all came to an end – I'm going to block those up, and then he must use the right passage and he won't be trapped.' He then did elaborate plumbing inside the hill. Somewhere in all this, he said 'Ding dong bell', and I said 'Pussy's in the well', whereat he gave desperate miaows.

Roger's next real communication started when he asked me to draw him; at the same time he drew me. About half-way through the important dialogue which followed he drew a second picture of me, and I did a drawing of him, which he liked. The third drawing he did on the last occasion that he came to see me in this series. It was as though he saw me for the first time as a real person and separate from himself, and this showed in the drawing. At this moment he said 'goodbye' to me and told me that he would not be returning. He did, in reality, look 'trapped' and he 'escaped' through my door – which, as it happens, is to one side of a wall. I did not interpret any of this because I felt that my room had become 'a hill' – in other words, the mother's body in which he had been trapped and out of which he had had to escape. It was not for several weeks that Roger wanted to come again, and his whole approach to me is now quite different.

After several relatively unimportant sessions, during which we played squiggles, Roger asked me once again to draw 'Mr Roger setting out'. This involved a drawing of him walking down a road which was left for him to continue down the pages of the block. The 'journeys' (as he now called them) always went from top to bottom of a sheet of paper and then continued over many pages, always from top to bottom so that ultimately the whole journey could be joined up (he never did this).

This journey took him to the coast; the route was clearly signposted and led up and down steep hills, across bridges and through a 'very dark wood'. He came at last to signposts, one of which said 'cliffs' and the other 'beach'. Here he hesitated and asked if I would hold on to him if he went and looked over the edge of the cliffs. I assured him that I would hold on to his heels, so he decided to take the cliff road. He reached the cliff-edge and became very anxious; however, he summoned enough courage to lie flat, looking over the edge, with me holding his heels. He exclaimed over the sound of the waves, the spray, the light and colour – all of which he described very vividly, so that I could see and hear also. After this achievement he was quite exhausted. He suggested that we should go down to the beach which was peaceful and beautiful. Then we went through another wood, on the edge of which he asked for a picnic. I drew him sitting with his picnic (he gave precise instructions – especially for tomato sandwiches). After the picnic which he enjoyed, he went to a town where there was a railway station and caught a train home (railway lines used to be an obsessional preoccupation).

The next journey some weeks later (after a holiday) took the form of a mountain climb. On this occasion he announced that I was to come with him. The first part of the climb was fairly easy, but became steadily more difficult. There had been a frost, and I mistakenly remarked that the rocks were slippery because of this. Roger was outraged: 'Don't be stupid, Mrs Dockar-Drysdale.' I apologized, and he said presently, 'You weren't really so stupid, after all, you have never been on this mountain before.' There were three hundred feet to climb, then one hundred, then fifty. We were getting tired. Suddenly among the rocks he showed me a small hut in which lived a kind old man and his wife, who cooked us bacon and eggs and so forth, and where we slept for the night. At dawn we climbed to the summit. Roger was now glowing with excitement. There was a flat, round place on top of the mountain. As soon as he had drawn this he *actually* climbed on his knees on to the round table at which we were sitting. He then planted a flag (in the drawing) on which he wrote 'Mount Roger'. I shook him by the hand, congratulated him on being the only person to reach the summit (I had waited lower down). Roger accepted my congratulations, rosy, bright-eyed and beaming with joy and pride. He had established his identity.

The latest journey also included climbing, but only a small hill in a part of Roger's country, not far from Mount Roger. As usual, I drew him setting out down the road when Roger took over, drawing the road with corners and signposts which would lead to the hill and on to the beach. For the first time, and to my great surprise, having drawn the first stretch of road he turned back to my drawing of himself in order to provide himself with a *large bag* over his shoulder (the capacity to contain experience). He said, 'You don't know yet what's in this bag, and you have no way of finding out!' I assured him that I could not know until he chose to tell me, whereat he smiled in a satisfied way.

He climbed the little hill without difficulty and then took the road to the beach, where he found a sheltered spot, where a stream flowed from a spring at the foot of the hill. Here he unpacked the bag and unfolded a tent, with food, cooking utensils and swimming trunks. He bathed, the sun shone, it was July, the sea was blue. Afterwards he was hungry and ate quantities of bacon and eggs. At last he packed his bag and went home, as usual by train.

Now, there is a lot that I could say about this material and its meaning, but for me – and I am sure for you – the important factor is the reality of Roger's experience in this symbolic form (again, what Sechehaye [1951] has termed 'symbolic realization'). This is a symbolization of early missing experience, which Roger had been given in the Mulberry Bush, mainly by Brigitte, and of his achievement of identity (the edge of the cliff and Mount Roger) following his symbolic escape from 'the trap' (the symbiotic tie with the mother) and the change from being contained to being a container (the bag he provided for himself in the drawing).

It is interesting to note that during this period he appears to have ceased soiling to any extent, although this had been an acute symptom for years. You will notice that I did not make interpretations to Roger, but only to myself. He was symbolizing experience for the first time: interpretation would only have reversed the process and made him find other symbols – to what end? I just accepted the reality of his journeys and accompanied him, giving support and encouragement when needed. He travelled through an inner world. This was something splendid, an adventure into life from the twilight wastes inhabited by people such as Roger.

Here is a very different confrontation with reality, where the theme was one of anti-life and the direction towards self-destruction and doom.

Roland was crouching, huddled up in a miserable little heap in the garden of the Mulberry Bush, one summer's day many years ago. A flue epidemic had just arrived, and nearly all the children and grown-ups were already ill. I thought that Roland was probably himself developing flu, so I sat down beside him, suggesting that he might let me tuck him up in bed. He shook his head and assured me that he was not ill – it was something much worse. Slowly it emerged that a few days before he had been very angry with everyone in the Bush, so he wove a spell – a cow-parsley spell, with a few minor additions which I forget. This spell was to make everyone ill. 'And it has worked!' he sobbed. We started to talk together about magical powers, about small boys who, unable to take steps in reality to punish their 'enemies', may believe that they have secret resources on which to draw – things like cow-parsley spells. I talked with him about how awful it is if a spell 'works', and how awful for a spell to fail: then magic doesn't exist and there is only a frightened unhappy child who is quite helpless. What a choice! We talked on together in the sunshine, and ultimately Roland settled for reality, and began to understand something about 'magic' and his own omnipotence and helplessness. He was an obsessional child, who guarded himself from annihilation by endless warding-off rituals – realization of reality would leave him totally vulnerable. Although this was a moment of truth, he withdrew behind his fortifications again and remained there.

I have said that Roland guarded himself against annihilation. The dread of emotional inner annihilation is infinitely more terrible than the objective fear of real death. Often an extreme terror of death in children and grown-ups alike covers the underlying dread of annihilation. We talk about 'separation anxiety', but this is often a euphemism to describe the fear of annihilation. Annihilation involves total destruction of the child *and* of the whole universe. Of course the child will not *really* be objectively annihilated; but his dread is real.

This is the zone in which it is difficult and frightening to accept another person's reality. A man whose wife heard voices speaking down the chimney when the wind blew at night assured her that *he* did not hear any voices – that they were not real. His wife became frantic, because she hallucinated voices, so that *she really heard them*. When a child claims that a room is shrinking or that he sees a man standing at the end of his bed, it is no use at all to say firmly 'but there is nothing there . . . everything is as usual'. What he is describing is real for him. We must accept his reality and preserve our own. The man I described in the first example could have asked his wife what the voices were saying; the child could be asked to describe the man at the end of the bed. Because it is very frightening to hear someone describe something which is not real for us, the temptation is to reassure – by denying the reality of the other.

When a child panics – with no visible cause – the most important thing we can do for him is to accept the reality of his panic; very often a grown-up with a panicking child 'catches' the panic himself, so that he loses his own reality and cannot reach out to the child in need. This acceptance of another's reality without losing touch with one's own is not an easy achievement and explains much of society's fear of mad people, but we do not have to go mad ourselves in order to be in empathy with them.

The mad child is one for whom reality has been too intolerable: just how much reality can children deal with? How can parents judge what is tolerable for them to realize?

I find myself thinking of two very different episodes. Brian, a seventeen-year-old patient of mine, told me that when he was aged about five his mother had given him a budgerigar which he loved very much. However, he forgot to feed the little bird and his mother found it lying dead in its cage one morning. She did not want Brian to face this tragedy, so she hurriedly replaced the dead bird with another; thus, it was not till years later that Brian knew what had really happened – yet somewhere within himself he *did* know. Now, in his treatment, he broke down into bitter tears of mourning and remorse, which he had been needing to reach for years.

The second episode concerned a small boy, four years old, named Peter. He was deeply attached to a duckling called Dilly. This duckling was killed by a fox one night, and with great grief his mother told him what had happened. This was Peter's first encounter with death, and he was appalled and wept for a long time. He tried to reassure himself – perhaps Dilly will come back? – but he himself refused to shut his eyes to the terrible reality. Ultimately he said to his mother, 'One day I may have another duckling but there will never be another Dilly.' Peter was given the support which was withheld from Brian. Children can stand reality if we can do so.

Children begin to perceive life through their parents' eyes – the more disorientated the view of the adults, the more impossible will it be for children to sort out what is dream and what is reality. The very disturbed mother of a boy of eight used to 'play' witches with him when they were out shopping together. 'Quickly,' she would cry, 'the witch is coming! Let's hide behind the letter-box.' The child was terrified and so was the mother, who was an emotionally ill person herself and was really afraid of witches.

If one is not living securely within reality oneself, one cannot help someone else to do so. Another mother hid in the dark behind the sofa for hours, with her little children, because, she said, 'The Germans are coming'. One father explained to me, 'When Guy says he can smell gas, we all say we can smell it too!'

Yet all these ill people may be saying what they believe to be real and true – they are communicating *their* reality, sometimes to their children, because they are the only ones who will listen.

And what about terrible objective reality which in itself seems mad, the awful things that human beings do to other human beings? How are children to come to terms with war, with murder, with torture? Perhaps the answer is by letting them know us as real people, as good and bad, as loving and hating, enabling them to tolerate the reality of being a human being among other human beings. If parents present themselves as always 'right', 'wise' and 'good' to their children, they are offering something delusional.

Illusion is fine for babies, but toddlers need to have reached disillusionment, to have come to know their parents as people who can get into difficulties – as the toddlers do themselves. There is a kind of mutual respect based on really knowing each other, which idealized, illusory parents will never reach with their families.

There is one vast area of reality which I must touch on, what I think of as 'the theory of the impossible task'. I have met this concept over the years in residential work with children, but I feel fairly convinced that it turns up in ordinary family life. People who work with disturbed and deprived children are encouraged to do so and described as dedicated and respected, on the basis that they are employed in attempting an 'impossible task'. Often the people who are doing this difficult and demanding work also believe it to be impossible (this can be the motivation behind their choice of work). They toil devotedly, accept teaching and advice, and understand theory, but the basic assumption remains – the fallacy of the theory of the impossible task. What is it that all these people feel to be **impossible?** I think they deny the reality of change – they do not believe that people can evolve in such a way as to make them *different*.

Consequently, when the task is seen to be possible – when, for example, a very disturbed child changes in every way, even in physical appearance – this success is not greeted with gladness and relief. Far otherwise, the change is felt as a threat; sometimes it is actually denied. There is a reason for this: if the child can change, then so can the adult – and adults will have their reasons for refusing to change. One can see this denial of the reality of the possibility of change in quite normal families, when parents find it difficult to allow their children to alter because of the challenge this presents: they insist that their children are as they have always been. Parents of disturbed children in treatment often deny the reality of the children's recovery long after other people have been able to accept changes of personality. If children feel that parents or grown-ups caring for them cannot see the reality of change in their personalities, they suffer, lose hold on identity, have innumerable doubts about themselves.

Babies and small children need an unchanging environment (one can think of the mother as the first environment). As they gradually establish their own inner reality, they can tolerate outer reality and all sorts of change – in themselves and in others. If all goes well, they can go on changing and tolerating change for the rest of their lives, but only if life has seemed more constant to them in that first year than it can ever be in reality.

Chapter 7

Realizations

I am going to try here to conceptualize certain realizations which I reached during 1976 while working as a consultant in the Cotswold Community. Richard Balbernie and the unit teams at the Community gave me a great deal of help by discussing the ideas with me.

Culture

Certain workers have particular functions and responsibilities at the Cotswold Community: they are known as 'resources'. Thus, there is a therapeutic resource, a continuity resource, an educational resource, a domestic resource. To these we added in 1976 a cultural resource. The word 'culture' is used here in a rather special sense, referring to every aspect of living, for example, laying of tables, pictures on walls, books to read, records to play. The garden and the workshop and the decoration of the unit are all included in the task of the cultural resource.

At first it seemed that this function was not going to operate, except in a very limited and superficial way. Then the cultural resource people and myself were asked to plan the decoration and furnishing of a large rehabilitated unit, a project which was carried out successfully, and with energy and imagination. Despite this small success there were no further developments. The term 'cultural resource' all but vanished. It was suggested that the function should be taken on by several members of a team. However, at this point we initiated group meetings of the cultural resource people with myself. There were five participants (one from each unit), all of whom made contributions concerning the progress of culture in their own unit, and they discussed one another's work with one another and with myself.

A representative of the school (which exists within the Community) joined the group, and from then on the cultural resource group became effective and important in the life of the place.

Perhaps the initial setbacks and indifference arose from an intuitive awareness that an active approach to 'culture' would set up a resistance among the unintegrated boys. Certainly this is what emerged. There was a typical reaction in Unit Four, which had only recently been set up and which was intended for fragilely integrated boys. Unit Four had been stripped down to its bones and then was re-created by the staff and the boys in a very imaginative way. Here the staff and the boys made the culture together, with the help of the cultural resource. All was well, there was no dirt, no destructive behaviour and at that time no subculture. Then three other boys joined this group; they were borderline people whom we thought would be held by the ego strength of the staff/boys group in Unit Four.

In the event, there was a brief honeymoon during which the newcomers were rather quiet and subdued. Their first step was to form a small subculture into which they could sink, in order to escape from the (to them) alien culture. They tried to set up a delinquent contract (about which I shall have more to say later) by which they would not attack the culture if the subculture could be ignored. There was no collusive anxiety around in the unit, so the subculture was challenged, resulting in a considerable and savage attack on the culture. This was quite open and was more an anti-culture than anything else. The culture held its ground, despite destructive behaviour and bitter hostility from the splinter group.

The task of Larkrise, this unit, as a living unit was on two specifically linked levels. Boys having reached a state of fragile integration needed to consolidate this wholeness and build up their ability to take an increasingly high level of responsibility both as individuals and as members of a group. The other part of the task was to provide an environment that could be enriching in terms of encouraging greater expression of creativity and imagination.

Both these areas of help seemed most clearly symbolized in a fairly self-sufficient environment where, in order to live, the group provided quite a bit for themselves and did not rely on a provider set-up. From the outset this was the basis of the culture and its beginnings were in involving four boys and five grown-ups in the conversion of a fairly dilapidated house. Gradually the group grew to ten boys and seven adults, and the house similarly reached a gradually more completed form. The investment in the group and in the identity which the project realized was very high, with the atmosphere of the group being that of a group able to work together for at least part of the time.

Actually to describe the culture, its feeling and atmosphere within Larkrise, is particularly difficult, since it is experienced mainly through an extensive range of day-to-day events, happenings, routines and actions. The idea of self-sufficiency is important in that it encourages greater responsibility and is something that everyone in the group needs.

With the task of re-building the house, which was the initial task, there was a high degree of investment because of the feeling of creating something unique and yet everyone being able to contribute to the way it was built up. The level of enthusiasm in both grown-ups and young people involved meant that we were attempting to put a quality into the building which could deepen the values and quality of life in the group.

In establishing the household, small gifts from people – a wooden bowl made by someone who lived in the Bruderhof community,* items from other households in the Community, furniture that was old, personal, wooden – all these began to express the centring of life in work, and to make statements as to how the culture was going to develop.

In almost every possible area we questioned how something should be built up: open-plan bedrooms, television in the kitchen, bookshelves in the toilet. Some things were decided only after living without for a period of time, rather than rushing to complete something that would be inappropriate later. Having a hole for a front door in the depth of winter for a couple of weeks apparently

---

* The Bruderhof was a German community dedicated to poverty and self-sufficiency. In the 1920s and 30s they lived in the houses occupied by the Cotswold Community today.

resulted in the kind of entrance to the house that we wanted, although we did not know what that was when we started.

Plants and the garden soon became a very important part of life and it needed a lot of laborious work to achieve our aims. With enthusiasm flagging now and then, somehow it was done, and the garden yielded most of our vegetables that summer and a major amount for the winter. Keeping bees, having to care for and provide winter hay for a donkey as well as fence a field and care for all the plants and creatures included in the household and its vicinity demanded increased responsibility and enlivened the life of the place, although dung-moving never became a favourite job.

Personal responsibility and the level of choice over television, deciding what time to put their lights out at night, as well as the contract to do with shopping and being responsible while not in the Community, all these and umpteen other smaller day-to-day actions and decisions encouraged individual awareness, and therefore individual responsibility. At the same time this worked to build group awareness and responsibility although that was by no means a smooth process, and at times seemed to run in reverse, and at a great speed.

In terms of the quality of living we aimed at many traditional aspects in the way of life in the house, traditional in the sense of something natural and alive rather than in the sense of institutional tradition. An occasional newspaper to which everyone contributes makes something of a more informal contact with parents. The level of reading, music, poetry, pictures, history, the value of each person and the contribution each makes to the household, these were the culture.

A higher level of self-sufficiency as a group fosters a high level of responsibility in each person. The use of everyone's individual skills and expressions adds both value to the culture and to themselves, and it is that which lies at the root of the task.

The delinquent contract

> They are playing a game, they are playing at not
> playing a game. If I show them I see they are, I
> shall break the rules and they will punish me.

I must play their game, of not seeing I see the game.

(Laing, 1972, p 1)

Perhaps R.D. Laing when he wrote this 'knot' was thinking about delinquent contracts, to which I have already referred. In many residential institutions for delinquent young people there is a scanty and inadequate culture, coupled with a virulent subculture. The delinquent contract lies in a tacit agreement between staff and clients to the effect that the young people will be polite and pleasant *providing that* the subculture is left untouched.

We found evidence of delinquent contracts in all units; however the unit cultures had become so strong (partly thanks to the cultural resource group) that the subculture was fairly weak. In one unit, as described above, some newcomers set up a new subculture, assuming a delinquent contract, but when they were confronted by the strong unit culture, a new phenomenon appeared, to which we gave the name of anti-culture. This took the form of an overt and violent attack upon the culture (including destructive behaviour) which put a tremendous strain on the ego nucleus of the unit. Ultimately, the anti-culture, collapsed and the splinter group was drawn gradually into the culture, which had stood firm throughout a long and savage attack. It is interesting to note that the original subculture did not merge with the anti-culture but reappeared at a later date in its original form.

I believe that delinquent contracts are the results of collusive anxiety in the staff, which can be relieved by a gain of insight. There was evidence of minor delinquent contracts in all units, which understanding brought to an end.

Smoking and delinquency

An interesting example is the question of smoking. In many institutions for delinquents there are many boys who are under sixteen but who wish to smoke (it is actually illegal to sell cigarettes to anyone below the age of sixteen). Since it is not possible for many of the boys to buy the cigarettes or tobacco, the custom was for an adult to buy the cigarettes himself and to sell these to the boys. Of course, looked at in the cold light of reality, this was collusion. Examining this phenomenon with the unit groups, I suggested that the custom should come to an end and that no one below the age of sixteen should be able *with permission* to buy cigarettes by whatever means – that, from then on, to buy cigarettes would be a *deliquent act*. After the age of sixteen, we could not, of course, forbid them to spend their money on cigarettes, but we would still warn these older people of the health hazards (by using films, etc.). At first there was uproar and resentment – 'You've always done it, why is it wrong *now*?' Ultimately in several cases a new contract was implicitly agreed. In Unit Three the boys shopped on Saturday afternoons – they used this opportunity to buy cigarettes from shops, which is easily done. The situation seemed to settle down, and there was marked unwillingness to 'stir things up again'. However, eventually the boys were told that if they were found with cigarettes they would have to do their shopping with a grown-up on Saturdays. This announcement led to rage, with massive acting out, for nearly a week. At the end of this period the anti-culture vanished (it is never sustained for long) and the subculture was weakened because another delinquent contract had been torn up.

The conflict regarding acceptance of responsibility in borderline integrated people

The task of Unit Three was to help borderline integrated people to evolve further into integration. This task proved especially difficult, and it took a long time before we realized the cause of the special problem in Unit Three. It was clear to all of us that the subculture in this unit was especially virulent and that boys who had made good progress in Units One and Two collapsed into delinquency in Unit Three. What we then realized was that the problem is one of conflict, and that this was in regard to the acceptance of personal responsibility.

There is no real responsibility in Unit One, where the adults are responsible. There is the dawn of personal guilt in Unit Two, where there is some evidence of reparation. It would seem that on arrival in Unit Three the borderline boys reach a sort of watershed. The conflict is between staying at a pre-personal level of guilt and progress to a fragilely integrated state, where personal responsibility is accepted, with healthy guilt leading to spontaneous reparation. Those boys especially in conflict stay on the unintegrated side of the watershed. They either form or drop into *a subculture where there is no question of guilt and reparation*. A subculture evolved for this purpose is especially strong and deep rooted. We found that there is value in surfacing this conflict – making it conscious to the group and to individuals. Furthermore, it seems to be essential that we should *expect* responsibility to be accepted, but it would appear that this must be done with adult support. For example, in the case of washing up in Unit Four, this could be arranged and carried out by the boys themselves, without grown-up intervention (at dinner time). In Unit Three this would not have been possible, but several boys *could* wash up *with* an adult.

In Unit Five, whose inhabitants are really integrated, we found that individual *personal* responsibility could be accepted. In the past this was asked of *the group* – and refused. However, it was noted that boys in this unit took full responsibility in most cases for their own sleeping area, so it was decided that, since there was still conflict in respect of responsibility, this should be required only of the individual. In the event this plan would appear to be sound.

It is hoped that realization as to the nature of the conflict experienced by borderline integrated people will make the difficult task more tolerable, and will also help the grown-ups to give support just where and when it is needed, so that gradually the acceptance of personal responsibility will be possible.

Discussing all this with the unit teams, I took the area of washing up as one in which one might be able to trace the development of responsibility in the Community. So, in Unit One the adults do the washing up, occasionally helped by a boy. In Unit Two, adults and boys do the washing up together – there are many occasions when the boys refuse to help. In Unit Three, the washing up is done on a rota basis including several boys and one grown-up. In Unit Four the boys do all the dinner washing up themselves, with *no* assistance from adults. In Unit Five, the washing up is done on an equal basis by boys and adults.

Newly integrated boys, whose integration has been reached through treatment, do not require the same management as do 'normal neurotic' boys who have achieved integration in very early infancy or in childhood. For quite a long period we tended to assume that boys reaching Unit Five were ready to be managed rather than treated by therapeutic means. This has proved to be a mistaken policy. The boys in Unit Five require treatment quite as much as those in other units. However, they need a different treatment from the other boys, because they have achieved integration.

There should be no question of a 'facilitating environment', no provision of primary experience, but, in their place, planned ego support, opportunities for functioning areas to develop and for non-functioning areas to come into action. Really we know very little about the nature of newly integrated people. But one can say with conviction that they tend to be paranoid – for this pronouncement there is plenty of evidence and the cause is not difficult to reach. Because their integration is so newly established, they are open to impingement and consequently need to defend the privacy of their inner world. As a result, they become suspicious, tending to project their own angry feelings on to an external persecutor. Since integration has been achieved they now have an inside and an outside – they have become containers, but their anger is too violent to be contained and so must be projected.

It is obvious that another task in managing newly integrated people is to give them opportunities to communicate their anger verbally. In this way they may begin to contain such feelings without feeling themselves at risk.

I referred earlier in this paper to the particular problem in Unit Five concerning the acceptance of responsibility. This difficulty is also concerned with new integration – the individual boy protects his newly found identity, so that rather than merge with other boys (as he might have done in the past) he keeps himself separate and distinct. This means that he can accept personal responsibility, and can respond to appeals to do so, but group responsibility feels alien to him, and we found that the boys in Unit Five could not easily be approached as a group until later in their evolvement. It was always hoped, however, that they could be responsible as part of a group before they left the Community. Premature pressure in this area leads to anti-social trends. I have always remembered one boy who had just achieved integration (having been frozen). He said, 'Please don't ask me to eat scrambled egg – I can't bear my egg to be mixed up with the others.'

Communication and dream (pre-logical) thought

In working as a therapist with deeply disturbed and deprived children and adolescents, I have made much use of the capacity for symbolic communication. I have not always understood, but I have usually been able to respond appropriately, using the same symbols as the child, so that eventually I have reached the hidden meaning. I am sure that most therapists, especially those working with unintegrated youngsters, have used this kind of communication. My concern is to establish *how* such response becomes possible without being unintegrated or schizophrenic.

I realized recently that this kind of communication needs a capacity for pre-logical thinking such as one uses in drawing. The question remained, *how* does one think in a pre-logical way without actually dreaming? I do not feel that we have reached a complete answer to this question. However, I can say with certainty that response to symbolic communication is not achieved by any kind of concentration. I find that I used to listen in a relaxed way but with the whole of me to what the child is saying. In this way I become acquainted with the symbols which he uses, and can respond in a relaxed, spontaneous way. I do not try to interpret the symbolic communication, but gradually as we go on I begin to realize the meaning of the symbols from the way in which the child uses them.

Years ago I wrote a paper ('The task of Larkrise', unpublished) on communication which started with a rhyme:

> The man in the wilderness said to me,
> 'How many strawberries grow in the sea?'
> I answered him as I thought good,
> 'As many red herrings as grow in the wood.'

I have written elsewhere (see Chapter 6) about many such communications, especially concerning 'Roger', a seven-year-old, who was especially gifted in the use of symbols. I have recently come to the conclusion that children *reach* symbolic realization (Sechehaye, 1951) when they make this sort of symbolic communication. The 'dream' – pre-logical experience – seems to them real, just as certain dreams do.

Chapter 8

Notes on selection

I had intended to deal in rather general terms with the problems of selection but when I finally came to write these notes I realized almost at once that the nature of such problems would depend entirely on the type of school involved; this being so, it seemed to me wiser to confine myself to a description of our own particular difficulties at the Mulberry Bush, in the hope that some of these might be sufficiently similar to those faced by other schools to make discussion valuable to us all.

Although I shall be discussing selection for admission to one special school for maladjusted children, it seems to me that many of the problems arising will be similar to those faced by teachers and others who are confronted with the problem of placing children in a school, a class or even a stream within a class. A move from one class to another – when this implies anything more than normal progress up the school – may be a serious matter for the child and for the family concerned. There are always two aspects to such a problem. The school recognizes the special needs of this particular child and makes suitable provision, to meet these needs. The making of this provision, however, will affect the child and his parents in all sorts of ways, according to the dynamics of the family constellation. What is most probable is that child and parents will see the special provision as an indication of failure rather than an opportunity for success and, if this attitude becomes fixed, the child will be immobilized and unable to make use of the provision in a positive way.

First published in *New Era* 41(8), September–October 1960.

The Mulberry Bush is a residential school for forty 'maladjusted' children, with two children to one grown-up. The children are all of about average intelligence, the age range being from five to twelve years. The aim of treatment is to return children to normal life as soon as possible. Usually this implies a return to their own family – in the case of deprived children, to a children's home, a foster home or whatever may seem appropriate.

There are four lesson groups, ranging from the 'smalls' – which has very little structure but provides deep early experience for the children in it – to the 'bigs' where there is very definite structure and from which children return to normal school life; these are the planned groups. There are also, of course, the spontaneous groups which are of great importance. Because of the way in which treatment is carried out, a deep bond is usually established between the lesson group and the teacher of that particular group, and it is then possible for this bond to come into every field of the child's life, because the teachers participate in every kind of 'caring for' the children. The whole team works extremely closely together and there is a great deal of mutual support.

I would like at this point to describe the exact practical process of selecting a child.

1   We receive a letter from a psychiatrist wishing to send a child to us, and giving us a condensed description of the problems for the child both as an individual and as part of a family constellation. *Note*: we tend, as I am sure all schools of our kind do, to select clinic and LEA as carefully as we do children. Also the psychiatrist and the LEA probably know us well.

2   We consider our current case-load and treatment team, and relate our present situation to the referred child. We find it necessary to consider the referral symptoms, release symptoms, treatment symptoms and recovery symptoms. These symptoms must be considered as far as possible in relation to the dynamics of the total situation, that is, in the adult and children's group (structured and spontaneous) during the next two years. I shall return to symptoms later.

3   We ask, ourselves what our aims would be for this child and

what the prognosis. How long a period of treatment would he need? How much would his family co-operate? Would he be able to return home on leaving us or would further placement elsewhere be necessary? If so, what form would this be likely to take?

4　We return to the present overt picture. What immediate extra strain would appear with his arrival – who would take this strain? For whom, grown-ups and children, would such a child be

    i　tolerable

    ii　intolerable?

5　How much help could we expect from this particular clinic? From the psychiatrist? From the psychiatric social worker? From the educational psychologist? Is this a clinic where changes of team are frequent? How much would this matter in this particular case?

6　Is the psychiatrist correct in assuming that this is a case for us?

7　What is the intellectual potential of this child? Is this adequate from the standpoint of therapy and communication? Does the educational psychologist consider the assessment of intelligence reliable? What are the educational problems? How far are remedial educational techniques going to help? Or is the educational retardation almost entirely emotionally determined?

Providing we are able to reach satisfactory conclusions about these fundamental questions, the next stage is for me to tell the psychiatrist that we can consider this particular child.

The clinic will then approach the LEA; this is followed by a 'go-ahead' from the LEA to us, and I visit the clinic and have a very thorough discussion with the clinic team on the total problem – the family constellation and this particular child. It is at this point that we begin to consider what will need to be provided *after* the child's stay with us in the way of further placement, or after-care, and follow-up. Some children also need to be admitted in the first place for a period of observation. This would be where there is doubt as to diagnosis.

We discuss our aims, what we can reasonably hope to achieve, be it much or little. We discuss the difficulties in working with this particular disturbed family and work out together the sort of team-work which will be needed, both in the unit and with the clinic. I put forward my ideas as to the kind of treatment approach likely to be needed, related to the sort of career this child is likely to have in our school, and the psychiatrist comments on this and makes suggestions and criticisms.

The psychiatric social worker and I talk over the parents' attitudes, both now and later (that is, following placement). We work out together a plan of how best we can work together as from the first interview, and try to gain some understanding of the roles which will be assigned to us, by parents and by the child.

The educational psychologist explains to me the educational difficulties involved, and we consider how best these may be overcome and at what stage of treatment.

I come back to the clinic, all being well, to meet the parents and the child. This is an important step, because the family will meet me for the first time on neutral yet familiar ground, with support from the clinic team whom they already know. Such continuity we regard as essential from the start. Usually I meet the family together in the first place for a few minutes, and then I have a therapeutic interview with the child, followed by a talk with both parents. However, should this be a case where it seemed desirable to interview the child with his mother I would, of course, do this.

My aim in the first interview with the child is to establish any kind of contact; actually, valuable material nearly always appears. With the parents I hope to be able to work through some of their fantasies about residential treatment (fantasies which range from very grand boarding-school to a colony for mentally defective children or prison). The psychiatric social worker has started this work, and I have some idea of what to expect.

I try to make it clear that it will be a team job – the clinic, the parents, ourselves; that they can *really* come whenever they like; that they do not have to send their child to our school; that I do realize how difficult it must be to send their child away; that our wish really is to return him to them as soon as possible, and so on. They usually ask plenty of questions and in answering these I am able to convey some of the attitudes of our particular team and the way in which we work. This, of course, also means warning them of the difficulties involved, the disadvantages as well as the advantages of therapy, the problem of having to do without a disturbed child, on whom they are often dependent because of their own problems.

Providing we have done fairly well, the child and his parents now come to visit us. At the clinic they met me on familiar ground. Now, although the school is new, they meet me again – here is one person with whom they have made contact. For both parents and child this seems to be important. They usually spend most of a day with us, see groups at work, meet most of the team as spontaneously as possible, have a meal with us and a further interview with me. The child will often like to have another session with me, or he may spend time with a member of the team, in or out of a group.

On these occasions we look at the diary together and plan the actual date when the child will be admitted. Whenever possible, and this is nearly always, it is the parents who bring the child to us. In this way he is to some extent coming *to* something, rather than just being sent away. Usually we suggest that this admission should be for a month in the first place.

Finally, the parents, or one of them at least, bring the child to us, and by now they do know us sufficiently to talk a little of their unhappiness, their guilt, their sense of failure, which are all likely to surface at this point and which, if not to some extent experienced now at a conscious level, may lead to panic a few days later or a demand for the child's return home a week after admission.

Not all our children have families and for these children it will be with social services personnel and with house-parents or foster-parents that we shall be working. The approach, however, will be roughly the same whatever the background.

We are quite clear that a child should *always* see the school to which he is going and, when occasionally (because of some emergency) we have consented to admit a child without the course of action I have outlined, the start of treatment has nearly always been slowed up through various unnecessary complications.

At various stages during this process, there would be team discussions about the various important factors which I have mentioned – the type of problem presented, the present and future symptoms, the kind of treatment likely to be needed, the stresses involved and who will meet them, the impact on us and on the groups. Will this be a 'honeymoon' child or shall we ourselves present 'a syndrome of first term despair'? The 'honeymoon' child will present no difficulties for quite a long time, but then there is an explosion; the child who evokes 'first term despair' will start off by behaving like someone who is quite mad, and will gradually turn into an extremely nice child – at the end of the first term this is difficult to believe. More than one or two such children during such a first stage cannot be tolerated at the same time.

Before illustrating these notes with case material I would like to return for a moment to symptoms and their influence on selection. It will be remembered that I made a classification of symptoms and I shall now enlarge a little on this system, starting with the remark that personally I am never very concerned with the disappearance of a symptom; my interest remains attached to the symptom, its new home and its next destination. Symptoms travel fast and it is as well to follow them as best we may.

Referral symptoms: these are those overt symptoms reported originally by Child Guidance Clinic teams and parents. There may be little resemblance between symptoms then described and those found on admission to a residential unit; this does not mean that referral reporting is at fault, but that there is nothing less constant than a symptom. Certain groups of symptoms, however, make such clear patterns that it may be possible to foresee something of the changes likely to take place during treatment.

Release symptoms: these are symptoms which make their appearance as the direct result of the shock effect of a therapeutic environment. They are often very dramatic, for instance, an apparently withdrawn child may suddenly become aggressive and destructive simply because he feels that it is safe to test the strength of the supporting milieu. Such symptoms will gradually give way to:

Treatment symptoms: these will be observed as the child slowly begins to use therapeutic facilities, whether by attacking them, leaning on them or using them in whatever way he may need at the beginning of treatment. These symptoms may change their overt form, the latent content (the meaning of the symptoms) remaining the same.

Recovery symptoms: these are the convalescent symptoms, which can be so difficult to manage that outsiders may say, 'He's much worse than he was on admission!'

It is usually perfectly possible to predict the 'symptom career' of a 'frozen' child (that is, one who is likely, unless he is helped, to grow up into a psychopath). Such a child is likely to be referred as delinquent, aggressive, destructive, stealing, truanting. His release symptoms will be these combined with storm-raising, merging with grown-ups and children, primitive extensions and with-drawals not to be mistaken for relationships (what we call at the Bush 'mirage transference') and other phenomena special to this kind of child.

The treatment symptoms in such a case will be panics and rages (due to interruption of his techniques), destructive behaviour, later a general unfocused depression, affecting his whole personality.

The recovery symptoms will be deep-focused depression (a state of mourning) following the establishment of a primary bond, psychosomatic symptoms, acute anxiety.

(Sometimes a symptom may appear more than once during treatment in its manifest form, the latent form, however, will have altered, and it is important to recognize and be prepared for such experience, which can otherwise be mistaken for a set-back. Stealing is a good example of this: to steal food from someone loved is a very different matter from 'pinching' from the larder.)

We find we can afford to have quite a large group of referred 'frozen' children in the Mulberry Bush at the same time, but only a few experiencing release and early treatment symptoms, because this is so disturbing to the main group of children and so exhausting for the team.

I have come to divide the disturbed children I meet into two broad groups, neurotic and pre-neurotic. It is from the pre-neurotic group that we select our cases.

When we consider neurotic children we can assume that they will need secondary experience; there must have been primary experi-ence for neurosis to be achieved (implying as this does the capacity to contain anxiety and guilt, and to make a transference).

Pre-neurotic children have suffered early emotional deprivation in some form; not having had primary experience, they cannot make a transference, they have not reached guilt or anxiety. They need to be integrated through primary experience with a therapist, who must *do* something for a child which would normally happen spontaneously to a mother and child during the first months of life. This is work involving synthesis rather than analysis.

Neurotic children can recover through the provision of a therapeutic environment with psychotherapy (in the classical sense of the word).

Pre-neurotic children need something rather different, namely the provision of primary experience. Such provision will include the opportunity for either a regression or a progression. Regression in this context implies total regression as described by Winnicott (1958). At the deepest point the therapist and the child may even reach that early stage at which a baby is still part of the mother. A child who can regress must have achieved *some* degree of integration; that is, have reached a point from which to regress. The regression group includes the 'caretaker selves' and the 'false selves', described by Winnicott (children who have built elaborate systems of defence at a very early stage in emotional development as the result of severe deprivation).

A progression pursues a different course since it is needed for the child who has never been able to separate out from its mother; there has been a traumatic break, but not a gradual separating. Such a child can only *merge* with another person; the progression is to integration and separate dependence with realization of boundaries to individual personality.

In the progression group are the 'frozen' delinquents whom I have written about elsewhere, and the 'archipelago' children – islets of ego growth in a chaotic sea of unintegration, our task being again to achieve integration, to turn the archipelago, as it were, into a continent.

It would be an impossible task to attempt to give a condensed description of such children here. What I shall, however, try to do is to report three initial interviews, showing how the three children concerned indicated their emotional needs to me.

Jill was a withdrawn child of average intelligence, aged seven,

institutionalized and conforming, adapting in the situation with me
to what she supposed I would demand of her. Presently, however,
when I suggested that we should play squiggles, she became more
lively and made my squiggle into a face. She then made a squiggle
for me, and when she pushed the piece of paper across to me I
remarked that it looked as though it was already something
definite, rather than just a squiggle. Jill smiled, took back the paper
and drew a second identical object beside the first one. I said that I
could see that there now was a pair, but this was all I could
understand.

> *Jill*: A pair of socks they are . . . baby's socks . . . one was lost.
> *Myself*: I am so very sorry – how cold the baby's foot must have
> been.
> *Jill*: Yes, they took her into a room with an electric fire and a
> television, but it wasn't any good.
> *Myself*: She needed the lost sock?
> *Jill*: It has never been found . . . will she ever find it?
> *Myself*: I am afraid not. I wish it could be so.
> *Jill*: Is there anything that could be done?
> *Myself*: Well, there is one thing which occurs to me. Could you
> perhaps learn to knit, and then you could knit another sock for
> the baby – but this would be very difficult, you would have to
> find a pattern and the right wool, and someone to help you to do
> it. There would be dropped stitches, and you might even lose the
> knitting and have to start once more.
> *Jill*: I would like to come to you, and to learn to knit.

This squiggle game told me a lot about Jill. Here was a child who
had achieved some degree of integration, and the lost sock
represented her earliest emotional experience, before she lost her
mother. The baby for whom she still needs the missing sock was
her own 'real little self' preserved and taken care of by the
conforming adapting part of her, which continued to function like
a rather strict nanny in relation to the baby part of her. It was to this
'nanny' part of Jill that I spoke, offering to co-operate in the
'caretaking' (helping her to knit for the cold baby). Although I
pointed out the difficulties involved, using the knitting theme as a
means of communication, Jill was prepared to accept my help.

This child is now, in fact, making a regression. The 'caretaker' part of her will hand over, if all goes well, to the therapist (in the way Winnicott describes) and Jill will become really herself – a helpless baby who has been waiting for years for such an opportunity. The sock which will really warm the cold small foot must eventually be knitted by the therapist.

The second child, *John*, was a 'frozen one' – a gay and lively boy, eight years old, out to charm me, chattering without a trace of shyness and giving little indication of the depth of his disturbance, except for the fact that it was by no means normal to be so much at ease with a total stranger nor to be so utterly unaware that he had any problems at all – despite the fact that I knew him to be a 'delinquent hero' who had already been in very serious trouble, the leader of a gang and the despair of his family and his neighbour-hood.

There was no suggestion of any sort of anxiety during this interview, but when somebody opened the door of the room in which we were working, John reacted with momentary panic: this was the only moment when there was any emotional tone in his attitude. He assured me that he could get along all right and needed no help from anyone. In fact, this boy had never achieved integration, his charm was a weapon which he used ruthlessly, he was absolutely without concern and had no awareness of bound-aries to himself – he merged with people and with his environment. For this boy a progression to integration was needed, and it would be a long time before he would be in a position to have experience, to realize it and to symbolize in the way which Jill could do so well. Indeed, he could not communicate with me in any real way, because he was unaware of our separateness from each other.

Note: this child, after a long and difficult period of treatment with us, has established his boundaries, is now dependent on his therapist as a separate person and is no longer delinquent.

The third interview was with *Robert*, aged nine, and at first I thought it would be impossible to establish any kind of communi-cation with him. He either sat looking blank or flitted about the room in a distracted sort of way. However, we started to play squiggles together and after a series of very disjointed bits and pieces we reached something very real in the middle of all the muddle.

This was, he told me, a very small mole, lost in endless passages under the earth, 'a kind of maze'. He went on, 'The mole does not know which way to go – up or down or where. He is terribly confused: there are so many passages . . . he is always getting lost.' I said that, perhaps, the mole needed something to hold on to.

Robert: 'A string or something, you mean? – But that would break.'

I suggested that there could be string that would be strong enough to hold. We went on from there, and just recently Robert told me, 'Mole has found a safe little place in the middle of all the passages.'

This is what I have described earlier as an 'archipelago child'. Although by no means as organized as Jill, Robert was much more a real person than John, even if superficially he seemed far more disturbed. But there were only bits of this real Robert which could be reached – a little mole in his labyrinth was one such integrated part of him.

By establishing and maintaining contact with the various islands in the 'archipelago' we hope eventually to be able to help Robert to unite the parts into a whole integrated person.

Although we may be able to predict fairly correctly the course of such cases and the order of events, this does not mean that we can time these events with any precision, although it is becoming easier to do this as our treatment approach becomes more exact. But there are all kinds of unpredicted factors which may turn up. For example, members of a clinic team may leave their particular clinic, for perfectly good reasons, and we may find ourselves the only agency looking after the family. It is very difficult for a new team to take over such a case.

We ourselves face the same problem and do what we can to solve it. An excellent therapist teacher worked with us for two years, leaving to take up a post abroad. Most of his group were successfully 'weaned' and established before his departure, but two partially thawed 'frozen' children re-experienced disastrous premature separation.

Another unexpected problem may be that part of a social history has never come to light, and may cause havoc at a later stage. For example, there may be another child in the family, boarded out in infancy and recovered by the parents suddenly during the time when the known child is with us.

Or it may emerge that mother has, in fact, had a previous marriage and another family, of which nobody knew.

Or a child, so disturbed as to be untestable, but assessed as average or above-average in intelligence, turns out – having stabilized – to have an IQ of 70.

Or father, who has remained a shadowy and apparently indifferent and vague figure in the background, suddenly intervenes, causing chaos in all directions.

Or, at the end of the first stage of treatment, the parents announce that their child has made a wonderful recovery and will now stay at home.

Or at the same stage they may say that the child is now much worse than when he came and must return home at once.

Or adoptive parents turn out to be the real parents and the whole case has to be looked at afresh.

Or the mother suddenly reveals to me at the end of a period with us, during which we have found the child very disturbed but *not* in the way described, that the description she gave originally was really of her husband, whom she did not feel she could discuss with outsiders.

Or, in fact, the child turns out to have an epileptic EEG.

Or we've all been wrong and he or she is really quite mad.

Or instead of the depression diagnosed, this is in fact a delinquent hero who was in a stage of 'hibernation' when referred.

Or a court mistakes an adaption for a recovery and rescinds a court order so that the child goes home much too soon.

Or a welfare officer finds the family a new house and assumes that all will now be well and naturally longs and endeavours to bring the family together.

Or one of us becomes merged with a delinquent, or over-involved in a regression, or over-identified with a child who feels persecuted.

There are, in fact quite a lot of odd things which can and do happen however careful we may be. On the other hand, we have found that planning does pay in most cases. If one or more unexpected problems do appear, on many occasions it is possible with good team-work to solve these – bearing in mind always that our aim must be to achieve primary emotional growth which will make secondary experience possible: only when this has been achieved can there be adaptation to the expectations of society, very different from adaption to the demands of the immediate environment which can happen without any primary emotional growth having taken place.

Chapter 9

Clinical material: contributed by staff members at the Cotswold Community and the Mulberry Bush School

The material which follows comes unaltered from the notes of several people working in the Cotswold Community and the Mulberry Bush School. These are examples of the provision of primary experience, and it is interesting to observe the contrast between *adaptations* to need and the provision of *transitional* experience. Briefly, one could say that adaptation to need is made by a worker and depends on the presence of that worker – no adaptation should be handed over to another worker. An adaptation depends on a primary bond between the worker and the child. A transitional object (Winnicott) represents the worker in his or her absence – both the real objective worker and the subjective inner reality of the worker in the child (Nick's pipe is an example) [see below p. 91]. There must be a relationship between worker and child for this to be possible, and the fact that Philip could contain Nick would suggest that the boy was on the verge of integration at this point. Adaptations are stepping stones to dependence; transitional objects turn up on the journey to independence. David's care of Alan's bears was really care of Alan, and felt by Alan to be care of himself. The notes of workers with such deeply deprived children are full of this sort of symbolic event and realization.

I have written concerning the particular kind of excitement experienced by delinquents, to which they have become addicted and which they describe during treatment. There are references to this excitement in the workers' notes, and part of the therapeutic process is to help the child to find his lost infantile greed, which has been displaced into delinquent excitement.

Alan (Cotswold Community)

Alan, the adopted child of a very rigid, undemonstrative couple, arrived at the Community laden with expensive clothes, toys and other belongings, which, by the lack of concern he showed for them, he sensed to be a substitute for rather than a symbol of the love which he had stolen from the child they never had. Only a very small, ragged, rather sad-eyed teddy bear which the mother had recently given him seemed to have any value for him. Within a few days Alan allowed me to look after, talk with and feed and play with 'Jimmy'. Alan told me that honey was what 'Jimmy' really liked so I bought him his own special jar from which we fed the little bear every bed time. It was important that I settled 'Jimmy' into his own bed each evening, that I rescued and looked after him when Alan lost him or threw him away – that I did not give up showing concern for 'Jimmy' even when Alan seemed to do so.

A little later 'Tom', a rather larger bear, was brought by Alan and he and 'Jimmy' had each his own particular way of eating honey. I had to make different noises for each bear and Alan told me, in consultation with his bears, how much each wanted to eat. A few weeks later a third bear was added, thus making a complete family. This last bear Alan named 'Minnie'. Quite often when I go into his room at bedtime, Alan is able to be the demanding, crying, shrieking, playful, inarticulate baby of the 'family' with me having to sense intuitively, as a mother does, his and his bears' needs for feeding and bodily comfort.

In the last few days, Alan has rejected his family so I have taken responsibility for them – adopted them, I suppose – until he wants them to return. **DAVID LOVERIDGE**

Stuart (Mulberry Bush)

Notes on adaptation and localized regression

3 October 1971 While settling the children I spoke to Stuart in bed. He reminded me that last term I had promised to find out whether he might have something special, an adaptation, this term. (Twice before over a fairly long period of time he had asked whether he might have cereal, and I had suggested we wait in order to find out whether there was a real need.) There was a feeling of quiet, calm urgency in his voice. He said that he had for a long time asked his mother for cereal (morning, noon, afternoon and evening) but she always refused saying, 'You've ate too much'. He said that his mother and father were talking about him 'stopping at home' after this holiday; so he wants cereal from me in bed 'for once': perhaps a feeling of this being a last chance.

The question of Stuart having a cereal adaptation was talked about with John and Pip. Stuart wanted sugar puffs with cold milk and, in talking it over with Stuart, we decided I should give it to him on Saturday and Sunday evenings in bed, after the children have begun to settle.

For four or five months Stuart accepted the cereal and my presence beside him as good enough. I would, for instance, support him with an arm around his back and I held the plate and bowl for him while he ate.

Mid-March (approximately) Then he began to make use of my sessions with him a more particular way; he would pretend to be 'asleep' and I had to wait for him to 'awake' before I could give him the cereal. This was the beginning, I felt, of a regression to dependence. In a later session Stuart pretended that it wasn't I who was there, and he wondered if I had brought his cereal. Although I had never failed him in this respect I had to accept his doubt, not reassuring him with 'yes' in order for him to work through towards trust. One evening when I arrived he began making the sound of an infant – a sort of cry – and I had to wait for this to come to an end (and protect him from the annoyance and curiosity of other children in the dormitory); it lasted perhaps ten minutes before he was ready to eat.

16 April 1972 Stuart was in bed awaiting me; I came with his cereal and when he saw me he turned over and lay as if asleep. I sat on the edge of the bed and stroked his hair. He twice turned his head in order that I should stroke both sides of his head and face. After a few minutes he turned on to his back and with his eyes closed he raised a hand and groped to feel my hand, and felt up my arm and to the features of my face. He then withdrew his hand. With his eyes shut tight quite obviously, he then groped with his hand to my side, and spoke for the first time.

'Where are you? Give me your hand.' I took his hand. 'Where is your shoulder?' I put his hand on my shoulder. 'Where is your head?' he asked and I put his hand on my head. It explored my face. He then asked to feel my other shoulder.

He then seemed satisfied and raised himself on his elbow, his eyes still shut tight and asked if I had brought his cereal. I didn't answer this directly because the question pertains to the question of trust. I replied, 'Are you ready?' and helped him sit up. I gave him the spoon which he'd asked for and he began to eat.

After eating several spoonfuls he stopped and said 'What is wrong with my eyes? They seem sticky. I'd better not blink or they might stick.' Then, 'Oh, they're stuck'. He brought the spoon up to the right of his cheek. 'Where's my mouth?' Clearly he wanted me to feed him so I guided his hand to his mouth. He then let me feed him several spoonfuls. He asked me to stop and rub his eye gently so that it might open. First one eye opened. He seemed uncertain about keeping it open, and I commented, 'It is like opening your eye to the world for the first time and you are uncertain about what you see. It is difficult to know whether you want to keep them open.' Shutting and re-opening his eyes once or twice more with my help he finished (feeding himself) his cereal, and at the end commented that I hadn't given him enough milk.

22 April 1972 There was humour present during my session with Stuart, and as an extension of the tactile experience (my tracing patterns with my finger over his forearm, for instance) he showed me the toddler's game of 'Round and round a circle, like a teddy bear, one step, two step, three step and I'll tickle you there' (under the armpit, begun with the forefinger circling round the palm of the hand), then he asked me to do it to him. Obviously he has already had some good experience from someone.

23 April 1972 Sunday evening (when I stay with him until he's asleep).★

He was much more matter of fact. He wanted tactile experience given him, e.g., the tracing or 'tickling' of patterns on his arm.

When eating the cereal he was 'messy' in a way that he hasn't been before, I felt. He pretended (I think) to get some 'puff corn' or 'pop corn' (sugar puffs) stuck in his throat; asked for some water he had in a beaker (providing for himself). This at first didn't dislodge the puff corn, so he said, and he said he would 'punch it out', he wondered what I would do if it would not move – but he didn't wait for or require me to answer. The trouble disappeared.

Not a great deal occurred during this period which seemed to be significant, except perhaps for two things which I had forgotten and later recalled. These two, described below, may or may not be linked and may or may not have occurred in the same session.

1 Once Stuart asked me to trace round his mouth with my forefinger many times. (I said 'asked' but usually the communication was non-verbal. Often he would take my finger and trace with it the pattern he wished me to continue tracing.)

2 One evening he had me trace patterns over his arm or around his ear (I can't remember exactly which area) before he had begun to eat his cereal. He was lying on his side in a regressed position and fell asleep. I waited for a long time wondering whether he would wake up and eat his cereal, but eventually it appeared that he wasn't going to wake soon, so I left him. (He could come and get me in the night if he needed me when he awoke. He did not do this.)

★ In explanation of my staying with him until he is asleep: after the second or third session of the localized regression was over, Stuart asked if I could sleep with him, or he with me, in a way that showed an urgent infantile need. I had to tell him immediately that it wasn't on, but that I knew that what he was asking me was important to him. I said I would talk about it with John and Mrs Dockar-Drysdale in order to find out what could be done. What was arrived at was this: on Sunday evenings I would remain with him until he fell asleep. This could happen only on Sunday evenings because on Saturday I was on late duty and could not devote myself completely to Stuart.

In the morning he remarked on what had happened and asked me why I didn't wake him up; he said he had wanted to have his cereal and didn't want to fall asleep.

14 May 1972 No preliminary regressed 'sleeping' to begin with. He had been talking with Stephen W. and seemed to feel a bit embarrassed or sensitive that Stephen was watching him with me. So he pretended to close a window between their compartments so that he'd have privacy.

He was in a playful mood, happy and open, security radiating from his face. He ate his cereal immediately with no games.

Afterwards he talked of many things though chiefly of a (father) gorilla ('Can they run fast? Could I [Stuart] run faster if it were chasing me?'). This fantasy comes into his mind in a real way, often in the transitional stage between being awake and falling asleep. This fantasy keeps him awake, he said. Sometimes the gorilla comes towards him but he walks around it and past it. The anxiety aroused by this fantasy seemed to be getting more tolerable. He then talked in a loving way about little monkeys.

I tried to ask him about transitional objects which he'd had to help him get to sleep when younger, but nothing special appeared to be recalled.

Later, he suddenly asked me about bringing his cereal. 'Would I bring it?' There was something insistent and hopeful in his voice and manner and after some doubt (unspoken to him) I went to fetch another bowl of sugar puffs and cold milk. He was delighted when I returned and playfully admonished me for being late, as though I hadn't yet been to him. I went along with this and in the same vein apologized and promised to try to do better next time. This time he ate more slowly and playfully, leaving the milk to the last and playing his game of trying to get all in the bowl on to his spoon, spilling the milk on to the plate in the process.

Session ended with my tickling his tummy the *way his mother does*, playing fire-engines 'ting-a-ling, ting-a-ling' over his tum with one finger. Finally he asked me to tickle his hand (palm) while he fell asleep. This was a good experience.

20 May 1972 A critical stage of conflict? During the eating of his cereal, Stuart suddenly rejected it, ordered me to put it to the side, and said 'It's gas' (poison) repeatedly. He insisted quite sternly on my taking it away even though I occasionally caught the beginnings of a wry smile at the corner of his mouth. The milk was very cold, so I exploringly enquired whether this was the problem. He merely said, 'It's gas'.

I wasn't prepared just to take it away, and he didn't indicate that the session was over and he wished me to leave, so I said that I had several more minutes I could stay with him, and that he knew the cereal bowl would leave when I did. He merely said 'It's gas'.

I felt very unsure about what he was saying and meaning, so I said so. I asked him if he could help me understand. I wondered about changing the milk ('It's off' he had said) but he said 'No – that wouldn't help.' By this time I thought his rejection of the milk might refer to the failure in his life with his mother. So I asked him if he knew what it was that was bothering him. He said 'No'. I said I had an idea what it might be.

'What is it?' he asked.

I felt that an interpretation was necessary if we were to proceed through this block. He was attentive, quiet and seemed to want some help from me, so I said, 'It seems to me that the difficulty lies in the fact that the first time something went wrong, and now [the second time] there is a chance for it to be put right.'

He made no reply to this, seemed to accept it. He was then able to accept the cereal and finish it happily and without conflict, finishing the cereal with his usual game of spilling all the milk from the bowl on to the spoon and on to the plate. He asked, 'Why is it that the milk seems all right now?'

Before I left him I pointed out that tomorrow (Sunday) would be the last session we would have this term.

21 May 1972 Stuart went completely under his bedclothes when I arrived, but almost immediately made a 'door' looking out towards me and asked, 'Is it the postman?'

Yes, I said. (He had played this game before although not in the same way.)

Stuart: Have you brought me a parcel?

Douglas: Yes.

He asked me to describe it, and I did so.

Stuart: What is it?

Douglas: A bowl of sugar puffs and cold milk.

Stuart: Where is it?

I made a game of this and said, 'Close your eyes and when I count to three open them.' The first time I got to three he opened his eyes looking over his shoulder. I counted again, and he looked up. Again, and he looked down. A few more times and he looked at his cereal, a big grin on his face.

He made room for me to sit beside him on the bed and invited me to put my feet in to keep warm. I declined to put my feet in, but he covered my lap with his cover and began eating his cereal.

While he was eating he began taking notice of a conversation among Stephen W., Mike F. and Martin, and kept looking from one to the other. This culminated in his taking part in the conversation briefly.

Then he asked me to read him a story from a comic while he continued eating the cereal. I did so, and he finished the cereal quite quickly, playing the spilling-the-milk-on-to-the-plate game just twice or three times before all the milk was finished. He had me put the bowl and plate aside and asked me to read another story. I said 'only one more' as it was getting late.

He wanted me to tickle the sole of his foot, then his leg. He was barely able to contain his mirth and excitement.

I said he would have to settle, so he said he would but asked me to tickle his arm which I did for a few minutes only. I had said that was all I would do, then I would just sit with him.

He was a bit restless and playful, at one point pretending to conduct music on the record. Then he turned over, sucked hard on two fingers for a few minutes, changed position once more and was soon asleep.

I think he may have reached, in six weeks, the end of his localized regression.

DOUGLAS HAWKINS

Jim (Cotswold Community)

It soon became evident after his arrival at the Community that through Jim and the excitement around him at mealtimes a message of a kind was being told. He was unable to accept any food like cottage pie, scrambled egg, porridge, and it was necessary to cook his food separately.* It was as if Jim lost any little identity of his

* He actually said that he could not bear his egg to be mixed with others (scrambled).

own when faced with this situation and just merged into any *delinquent* excitement or led others into it. He needed firm male support and containment at these times. With this structure Jim was able and wanted to accept help with his problems. He was able to gain insight into these feelings and was helped by the leader and his team to accept and conceptualize the idea of having as many apples a day or night as long as he felt it was necessary. During this time Jim and the adults involved were helped by our consultant to gain the insight he needed and worked through a lot of his feelings of rejection towards his mother, the deprivation he had experienced in his early years, the feelings of his own hospitalizations, the feelings surrounding his mother's death and the lack of concern from his father. But because Jim had had so many incomplete and interrupted experiences this gave him an opportunity of a complete experience. The demands for apples were intense the first few days but this lessened and Jim would ask when he needed them or felt he would and they were always accessible for him. He always asked for two to be at his bedside at night time. He weaned himself off his apples and during the weaning process he asked for cheese on toast, which was made available for him. But by this time Jim had enough trust and confidence in the adults around him that he would receive this that he did not make immediate demands, but would wait for its arrival, often checking that it was being cooked but not in an excitable or aggressive way.

MARGARET LEAKER

John (Cotswold Community)

John came to me one day and talked to me about how he did not want to get caught up in delinquent excitement, but that there was a little man inside him who sometimes went away and when the little man went away he seemed to have no control over himself at all. The little man seemed to be John's self, so I told him that we had to find a way of helping the little man inside him grow bigger and stronger, so that he would not get frightened and go away. If this happened perhaps John's own violent bit would be more controlled.

We bought a small model of a very angry looking Red Indian (representing John's own violent bit), put this Red Indian inside a box, and locked the box, then the key to the box we placed inside an Airfix model of the yeoman of the guard, his own aggression (the Red Indian) being put inside the control of his self (the yeoman of the guard). After we had finished this, John said, 'Already I feel stronger and one day I will not need the yeoman of the guard to look after my anger, because I will be able to look after my own anger, won't I?'

Although after this there were still one or two outbursts, after a period of about six months involving a very firm management programme provided for him by the male members of the staff together with sessions with myself, John seemed much calmer and in control of himself. He was able to communicate well and look ahead to situations which would cause him the sorts of stress which could induce an outburst and come to me to help him look for ways of helping to prevent this happening. He said one day 'You know Christine, I really don't feel that I need the yeoman of the guard any more. I can look after my own temper; but just to be safe we are keeping it there and reviewing the situation in three months.'

CHRISTINE BRADLEY

Philip (Cotswold Community)

Provision of safety – a secure environment – has presented itself as a major factor in working with severely damaged and deprived children. A containment of angry or violent, often terrifying feelings can be provided for in relationship with an adult who is present within the living group. The absence of that adult for even a short period can often mean a complete loss of the security an individual needs.

Philip's previous experience had lacked any form of safe containment when feelings insistently took over and became sudden frightening action. Feelings of accusation and blame on occasions resulted in his attacking the person he felt to be threatening him. These incidents were 'fugue'-like in character and his recall of them difficult.

Having been within the unit for some months Philip began to find safety in relation to myself and expressed this. However, my absence from the group at one period prior to this expression resulted in several extremely excited and violent incidents, which I directly relate to the lack of a safe person for him.

The one object which he most connected with myself, and constantly referred to, was my pipe, and I at first began by giving him my pipe whenever I was going out of the Unit. He would solemnly return it to me when I came back. Initially, he carried the pipe in his hand or pocket, then he progressed to placing it in his bedroom, returning to it constantly almost as reassurance, and finally to almost total unawareness of its presence. It was quite noticeable that, as he became used to this simple provision and communication, the tension lessened during my absence, and on no occasion from that time did he lose control while I myself was not physically present.

The final communication in relation to this piece of provision was that Philip described going home for a weekend and being unable to sleep or even get into bed in his own bedroom, yet when he had placed the pipe, which he had forgotten he had in his case, on the dressing-table, he felt able not only to relax but sleep soundly, something he had found acutely difficult at home for over three years.

NICK BENEFIELD

Chapter 10

Bringing the symptom and the patient together

Often, in the course of my work, I am asked by parents or by staff in residential places, or by children themselves, to do something about a symptom. I am brought such a particular symptom either by the person to whom it belongs or by a person or people who are affected by the symptom. In both cases the symptom is usually quite detached from the *person*. An obvious example of this separation is to be found in bed-wetting and soiling. I am told about ruined mattresses, endless washing, smell, and so on, or alternatively about solutions – bells ringing at the first drop of urine, special rubber sheets or nappy-like contrivances to avoid the wetness spreading. Sometimes I am told about elaborate systems of rewards and punishments, but even then one gets the feeling that everybody – including the child – is ignoring the psychic importance of this symptom for the child, and his need to *have* his symptom, and for us to contain him-and-his-symptom, which is really part of him. (A colleague pointed out to me recently that people speak of a child wetting *the* bed, rather than *his* or *her* bed.)

From my particular point of view, the bringing together of the child and his symptom is often the first and most fundamental step in his treatment. Should we fail to help him to achieve this bit of integration, we are likely to build up a recovery round a hole – whatever the symptom may represent in the child's experience.

A very striking example of how this can happen was the case of James, who had a very rare tic which was verbal and took the form of obscene words, uttered in an explosive and quite uncontrollable way. He came for treatment to the therapeutic boarding-school for disturbed children where I work, and at first we wondered whether we could possibly keep him, because his jerked-out obscenities proved so disturbing to both grown-ups and children. However, the problem evolved into something quite different – grown-ups and children became so accustomed to James's tic that they ceased to notice its presence. James recovered in all sorts of ways, became less anxious and more able to be normally aggressive, was less depressed and made good relationships with men and women, but the tic remained and presently when we spoke of his recovery and achievement we had to remind ourselves that in the middle of all this development was the tic – quite unchanged and felt by James and other people to be separate from the rest of him.

I have had for some time in treatment a lively and charming boy of twelve whose main symptom was soiling. The soiling was excessive and happened at any time of the day or night. There had been a conspiracy of silence among the family, who were devoted to him – garments and bedding were washed, the soiling was played down in discussion with me and was regarded as a phenomenon which could not be explained and was best ignored on the basis that 'he would grow out of it'. I have been trying to help Thomas to claim his symptom.

Thomas himself remained quite detached from his soiling. He hid soiled pants, but not from guilt, in the ordinary sense of the word. Once they were hidden – just carelessly in a drawer or box, under the bed – they ceased to exist for him.

During our sessions together Thomas talked about himself in a very insightful and sensitive way, but he never made any reference to the soiling and I was especially anxious that it should be *he* who chose to mention this trouble.

It would have been easy for this to have continued and for Thomas to have made a superficial recovery round the symptom of soiling – he had other problems in the fields of eating and learning. My main task was in some way to bring him and his soiling together, and this has taken quite a time. Since Thomas never spoke about his soiling, I decided that perhaps what I could *do* might be more important than anything I could say to him. I felt that we were concerned with matters which belonged to the beginning to his life, and that his parents' separation and his divided loyalties probably produced a situation for him which repeated this early difficulty.

Accordingly, I tried to provide him with satisfactory experience which must somehow have been missing at the beginning, so I always washed his soiled pants myself – with concern – and he often saw me doing this, and knew that I did this from choice, and because I cared for him. (When I brushed his hair he said, 'You do it as though you mind how I feel.')

Although he did not yet refer directly and verbally to the soiling, he stopped hiding his pants, leaving them on the table in his room for me to find – where he could still *see* them, rather than throwing them into a drawer or under the bed so that they could cease to exist for him, on a basis of 'out of sight, out of mind'.

He also talked in his sessions about the good experiences his mother gave him about which his father must not know, and vice versa. I observed that it sounded as though he had to be *quite empty*.

A few days later he brought back a large 7 lb empty sweet jar which he had bought with his own money. He was washing this out next morning when it was time to go to school, so I offered to finish the job. (There was a little sugar at the bottom – he needed the jar to be empty.)

He accepted my offer and, having completed the task, I bought 7 lbs of sweets and *filled the jar*, putting the jarful of sweets on his table, for him to find on his return from school.

I happened to be nearby when he made this discovery: he could not believe his eyes, kept murmuring, 'But it's real' and fetched other people to confirm that the jar was really full of sweets. We knew I had done this, but we did not have to say anything to one another – we both knew this was important at a pre-verbal level.

Presently, some days later, when he had eaten and shared most of the sweets, he put the remainder in a small box, made a slot in the lid of the jar and began a collection of *sixpences*. He told everybody about this collection, which is growing; both parents give him sixpences and these are all together safely in the jar. At the same time, soiling has practically ceased and he is also putting on weight (that is, making more use of food inside him) and enjoying his meals in a way which is very different from his earlier attitude to food. In a dream he caught three fish – one big, one middle-sized and one small – all of which he cooked and ate (his father, his mother and his brother). In parallel with all this, he began for the first time to concentrate and to learn with pleasure for long periods.

Now there is a great deal which could be said about this material, but I want to consider only certain aspects. Here was a boy who could not contain experience, which for him was food turned into faeces. He had to preserve the experiences by hiding and disowning the soiled pants. He also denied responsibility for accepting good experience – food from either parent. He knew nothing about it and *kept himself empty*.

Because I was not involved in the struggle and was felt by him as a fairly safe person, he could allow me to fill the empty jar (= his body). The sweets and good experience (= food) then turned into money (= faeces), but now he felt it was safe to *keep* something in the jar, and furthermore he could keep what *both parents gave him*; at the same time he accepted responsibility for his bodily functions, for eating and digestion and excretion, incorporating what was of value to him and eliminating what was not. The slot in the top of the sweet jar became his mouth and the open top of the jar (turned upside down) his anus. Now at last he is talking about his soiling and all the many symbolic aspects of the symptom, which is felt to be part of *himself*.

The phenomenon of panic is another example of a symptom separate from a person. A nineteen-year-old patient, Anne, suffered from terrible panics which overwhelmed her in any place or at any moment. These panics were felt as attacking from outside (as I think is true of all panic, however brief and slight).

As the result of long and difficult work together, we have reached a stage where most of the panic is back inside Anne, because we have been able to understand what physical experiences the panic represented. For example, there were breathing difficulties when she was a premature baby which remained as one kind of panic in which she felt that the room was closing in on her. Insight into the history of this particular panic produced a brief attack of asthma (which was what I would call a recovery symptom).

The panics are becoming more and more localized as she

becomes more complete, having collected back the missing bits of her, as it were, which she had disowned. She is transformed and is felt by herself and others to be a 'new' person.

I have mentioned an attack of asthma in this case, where the symptom was transitional, a half-way house from the panic. A small boy, Tony, is a chronic asthmatic, with a very male, omnipotent and smothering mother; his father left the home shortly after Tony's birth. This little boy, dominated by his mother, never dared to feel anger or express his resentment and rage against her. Once when he had a very bad attack of asthma, which confined him to bed, I came to see him. He was choking and spluttering in a frantic and desperate way, and I realized that he was swallowing all the phlegm. I said there was no need to do this, and that I thought it would help for him to spit. He said, 'I've always had to swallow it', and I realized he referred to his rage. I told him he need do so no longer and showed him that he was really talking about *anger*, with the result that he spat for about five minutes – all over me, his bed, everywhere – and then screamed with rage, ending up in floods of tears, but in my arms and relaxed.

Recently his mother sent him a pair of girl's trousers. He was terribly upset but said to me, 'I can be really angry about this, can't I?' He still has asthma, but not nearly so often nor so severely.

This kind of symptom, that is psychosomatic troubles, can very easily be treated physically, having lost all connection with the basic cause of the trouble.

One often hears said – and rightly – that we are concerned with the whole person, not just the symptom, but there is also the danger of treating the person *apart from* the symptom, and in ignoring the symptom we may reinforce the child's split from what is really part of himself. Thus, if we were to ignore Tony's asthma and try to understand his emotional difficulties in a different and separate way, we might easily find ourselves thinking of the asthma as a *medical* problem to be dealt with by physical means (drugs, injections, etc.). What would happen only too easily would be that the asthma would be cured, which would mean that Tony would have to settle his rage in some other field, where it would probably turn up as another physical symptom, or as a tic, or as soiling.

In the same way, it may be necessary to give a child sleeping tablets for insomnia, but it would not be sound thinking to regard such a step as a cure for insomnia.

I have said nothing so far about delinquency and destructive behaviour. Many children steal as though they were sleep-walking; afterwards one finds that they remember very little about the actual act of stealing. They remember a rising tide of excitement and then they detach themselves from their moorings – that is to say, from all feelings of guilt or personal concern. If we merely punish them for such actions, we remove any chance of their reaching guilt; what we really need to do is to re-connect, or connect for the first time, this bit that can steal ruthlessly to the other parts of them.

Recently I suggested to a delinquent boy, Brian, that he should keep an eye on himself for a few minutes. He replied, 'That's something no one can do. No one can keen an eye on themselves – grown-ups have to do that.'

Destructive behaviour can also very easily be split off, and we may help to perpetuate this split. Arthur used to have phases of window-smashing. We found, after a lot of patient discussion with him, that he was trying to break through the barrier of silence which he felt separated him from his mother. He had this feeling when he had not seen her, had a letter or heard her voice for some time, and imagined that she was dead. By arranging and paying for weekly phone calls from his mother to Arthur, we were able to stop the window-smashing, but only because Arthur was helped to feel his rage and despair. You can see that, had he been punished for breaking a window, no link would have been established with what was inside him.

Many of the most serious and distressing symptoms that we meet in our work with emotionally deprived children are present because the child has been unable to tolerate *a feeling* so this has been turned into some form of action, either partly (asthma) or wholly (stealing) outside himself. Many of the feelings (rage, despair, terror) have been first experienced at a pre-verbal stage, so that the anxiety is unthinkable (Winnicott) and the feeling cannot be contained.

This is what I am thinking about when I suggest that our main task may often be to unite the child and the symptom.

Chapter 11

The process of symbolization observed among emotionally deprived children in a therapeutic school

My aim in this paper is to isolate one particular process, 'symbolization', from the many complicated processes through which children are moving on their journey to integration as individuals. In our therapeutic school for disturbed children, we have come to speak of the particular group we are trying to help as emotionally deprived (rather than simply maladjusted or disturbed), in as much as that these are children who have had gaps in the continuity of their existence at the beginning of their lives.

We are thinking in terms of a series of processes which must be gone through in order to reach integration. These are experience, realization, symbolization and conceptualization. By this I mean quite simply that a child may have a good experience provided by his therapist, but that this will be of no value to him until he is able, eventually, to realize it; that is to say, to feel that this good thing has really happened to him. Then he must find a way of storing the good thing inside him, which he does by means of symbolizing the experience. Last in the series of processes comes conceptualization,

First published in the *New Era* 44(8), 1963, and reprinted in R. Tod (ed.) *Disturbed Children*, Longman, 1978.

which is understanding intellectually what has happened to him in the course of the experience and being able to think this in words: conceptualization is only of value if it is retrospective – ideas must be the sequel to experience. There are many people who have had to substitute ideas for experience, who then try to force subsequent experience into the Procrustean bed of an organized system of ideas. Even coming straight on the heels of emotional experience, conceptualization is premature and arid. These other processes, realization and symbolization, provide the essential stepping-stones to what, after all, conceptualization really is, an economic method of storing experience and at the same time establishing the means of communicating experience. It is not enough to give emotionally deprived children good experience, we must also help them to keep the good things inside them, or they will lose them once more.

Babies who have 'good-enough' mothers are able to proceed at their own pace from experience to conceptualization. The emotionally deprived children who come to us for treatment have not had 'good-enough' mothering. The first year of their lives has been interrupted by disaster, there are gaps which have never been filled and they lack the necessary experience for which to need storage space. They are not, of course, aware of this – 'you do not miss what you have never had' – but when children have had primary provision of the kind I have described, they achieve realization and frequently express their difficulty in finding storage in their minds for their new experiences.

In the Mulberry Bush School we attempt to evolve a therapy of provision; we try in a therapeutic milieu to fill these gaps at the beginning of such children's lives. In this paper, however, I shall be talking not so much about the nature of the therapeutic provision which we make for the children at the Bush, as about the means they use to store what we provide through the use of symbols.

David said to me, 'I haven't room inside me to keep the memory of all the things that have happened to me here.'

Maurice said (showing me a procession of animals, wild and tame, at the beginning of a book of fairy tales), 'How can I have wild lions and tame cows inside together?' (his love and his hate).

Sefton said, 'I need a box inside me to keep things in that have happened.'

Robert said, 'I can't keep all the words about all the things inside my mind, there just isn't room, no one could remember all that. 'I here must be another way of keeping what I remember.' The 'other way' to which he referred is symbolization.

Now and then a very disturbed child may be referred to us who has integrated in some areas, and has been able to contain, realize and symbolize some emotional experience, even though this has been traumatic.

Robert in his first session with me drew (from a squiggle) a staircare. Half-way up the stairs there was a gigantic step. When asked 'How could anyone climb that step?', he replied, 'I couldn't – it was too big – what can I do?' I suggested (trying to communciate with him in his own symbolic language) that he might be able to build a small ladder, which would enable him to go on up the stairs, but that I thought nothing could be done to alter the step. He accepted this proposal and asked me to help him to build the ladder. Here was someone who had a traumatic gap in his experience, who had realized this and had symbolized the experience, and contained the symbols in a form which could be communicated. Had I asked him, 'What do you think went wrong when you were little?' he could not have told me. Actually, Robert was very small when his brother was born, and his young and inadequate mother felt quite unable to look after two babies at once, so she gave the new baby all the primary experience at her disposal, at the same time cutting off adaptation to Robert's needs and depriving him of the final stages of integration. This was the 'gap' – this was the gigantic step in the staircase which he could not climb; but he was able to tell me about his problem because of his capacity for symbolization.

Recently I met Jacqueline for the first time. She was most unwilling to have anything to do with me, hid behind the chair, covered her face with her hands and in various ways mimed hiding from me. Presently, however, we found that she would like me 'to call her on the toy telephone'. I asked – when at last I got the right number – from where she was ringing, and she said 'Behind the tree in my garden!' The telephone conversation continued, and Jacqueline gradually started to talk about herself in a way which I felt she might regret later, because I was sure she was not intending consciously to trust me with such information. So I said, 'It sounds to me as though you are coming out from behind the tree in your garden.' Jacqueline was furious and screamed, 'You shouldn't have said that – now I'll go right over the garden wall.' I said that she was quite right to go over the wall, but if she came back into the garden I would know she wanted to do this, and was not just coming by mistake. Presently we re-established our discussion on this new basis. Here again this child, who was very mistrustful of me, was able to convey her attitudes and to open a field of communication with me. She could certainly not have had the conscious insight to conceptualize these attitudes, to understand the complex cross-currents of feeling which she was experiencing. Nevertheless, she *realized what she was feeling symbolized* her fear of me and was, therefore, in a position to *tell me* about her panic reaction to my words.

Sometimes one sees very clearly that a child may be driven to acting out in the environment because he has been unable to symbolize, so that acting out *in a symbolic way* becomes the only means of communication apparently available to him. This is a very common reason for the wild outbursts of destructive and aggressive behaviour which one associates with disturbed children.

Porky had been slowly approaching complete integration as the result of the continuous care of his therapist (Vanno Weston). The crisis occurred when two newcomers were introduced into Vanno's group, an event which all too faithfully reproduced the birth of the next babies in Porky's family. He broke down into chaotic and destructive behaviour, doing everything he could to produce a state of stress so acute that Vanno would refuse to keep him in her group. (In the original disastrous situation he had been sent to a children's home for a period.) It was possible for Vanno and myself to make Porky see what he was doing unconsciously, and I told him that he might find it possible to help Vanno to look after the new members of the group, which he had never been able to do in the original context with his mother and the babies. (Vanno has asked him to help her to look after a bowl of bulbs for her, which will be a symbolic means of identification with her in caring for new life). Porky broke down into a frenzy of acting out through a failure to symbolize traumatic experience in the original situation, and a subsequent inability to communicate his suffering in any socially acceptable form, in a context which felt to him like the original trauma.

Perhaps this is the place to try to say something about 'sublimation', and to compare this concept with symbolization. I think it might be true to say that symbolization is the first step *towards* sublimation; but that symbolization is a much easier and more primitive mechanism. Symbolization can be used, as we have seen, in plenty of ways, but I think the aim of symbolization remains constant – that is, *to store a realized experience in such a way that this can be preserved and, if need be, communicated.* Remember, however, that all the early important experiences happen in the baby's life *before he can speak.*

I have spoken elsewhere about adaptation to individual needs, and the kind of symbolic adaptation which turns up in the provision of primary experience also aims at giving the child localized experience in a symbolic form, which can be stored by him. The form the therapist uses for such an adaptation must be acceptable to the child, but nevertheless, when he subsequently *realizes* the experience he has been given through the adaptation, he may make use of other symbols in order to store this experience. One could say quite simply that symbolization is a way of keeping things which could not be kept in any other way.

Sublimation, however, is a more mature process, involving a change of *aim.* There must be a really integrated person present for sublimation to be a relevant concept, a person capable of making identifications. Such a person will have had experience, realized, symbolized and conceptualized, and will have gone on to identify with important people in his life (his parents or parent figures) and to have aims other than relieving instinctual tensions. He is now able to make use of instinctual drives, harness them, and redirect them to help him to achieve his aims. What often happens of course is that people 'displace' (aggression for example), but displacement does *not* imply a change of aim.

Let us go back to Porky and the bulbs. Vanno, you will remember, is going to ask Porky to help her *to look after a bowl of bulbs.* You can see how different this will be from a situation in which Vanno might *give* Porky a bowl of bulbs or where Porky might attack Vanno's bowl of bulbs (perhaps pull them up and destroy them). I want you to think of these three possibilities in terms of Porky's present and original problem. There were the babies his mother bore after him, and in the same way the new children whom Vanno has accepted recently into her group. (Of course, a bowl of bulbs could be used in quite a different way in another emotional context.) Traumatic experience which has not been internalized, realized, and so on, will be likely to be repeated: that is to say, the child will always be meeting situations which will feel the same as the original trauma. Our aim in treatment is to help him to deal effectively with such traumatic re-experiences and to complete them in a creative way.

If Vanno were to give Porky the bowl of bulbs she would be saying, in a symbolic way, that Porky could be the father of the family represented by the bowl, herself (the mother figure) and the bulbs (the babies). This would be by-passing the current problem and facing Porky with an even more difficult dilemma – that of having been allowed to steal the father's rights, in other words Vanno would be in collusion with Porky in obtaining, albeit symbolically, satisfaction to which he would have no right. She would be putting herself in a false position. If Porky were to destroy Vanno's bowl of bulbs he would be displacing his rage against Vanno and the babies – the new children. It would obviously be better for the bulbs to be destroyed than for Vanno and the children to be hurt, but there would be no change of Porky's aim, which would remain destructive. However, by asking Porky *to help her to look after the bulbs in the bowl*, she is enabling the child to symbolize his realization that, although he is no longer 'the only baby' or 'the newest baby', nor the father of the family and, therefore, Vanno's husband, nevertheless he has his own place in the group-family, and can identify with Vanno's care of the new ones because she has helped him to find symbols and to use them in a way which will help him, so that his experiences can become creative and growing rather than traumatic and interrupting growth as they were originally. The cruelty which he might have shown towards the children or the bulbs can now, through his understanding of Vanno's feelings, become changed into pity and a wish to protect the young and helpless, in just the way that toddlers are helped to change their cruel feelings towards the new babies into compassion and care because their mother enlists their help, making it possible for them to identify with her aims, so different from those of the toddlers.

There is a tremendous amount more to be said about sublimation, but at least one can see from Porky's treatment situation that one can symbolize, or duplicate in a symbolic way, without sublimation taking place – that it therefore matters very much how one uses symbols.

The next child I want to talk about is David. He is of good average intelligence and is nine and a half years old. Recently he came to see me and found me writing the beginning of this paper. He asked me questions about what I was writing and, when I had answered him, remarked that he would like to write something of the sort himself – about the work being done for children at the Bush. For various reasons which we can consider later, I suggested that if he could do this I would be prepared to have his 'essay' typed inside my own and read it with mine. I only wish to make one comment before I give you his essay, which is that this child has only survived emotionally through his ability *to conceptualize immediately following experience*. He is a boy 'full of ideas' as you will see: he makes, however, no use of symbols, and until recently he intellectualized everything, to the exclusion of feeling and realization. Whenever feeling broke through this intellectual defence he panicked. He has recently been through deep primary and 'gap-filling' experiences at the Bush, and some of these have been in key sessions alone with me, although many others have been with Mildred Levious, who looks after his group. I have been the supporter in this case, but have been used more directly than usual by the child.

Essay about the Bush – by David

People have come to understand things at the Bush, that need help. And, some people found it difficult without the Bush. And sometimes they find it difficult to understand about it. And it is more easier to understand in the country. Sometimes they need help because their mothers died when they were little babies and sometimes they found it difficult to learn at other schools – like me over sums what I found difficult. And sometimes they've come to the Bush so that they can start their things all over again so they can remember.

And when they leave the Bush they may find it easier when they are learning at other schools, and sometimes they've come because they've got into a lot of muddles, and so that they can get the muddle undone; like getting knitting that's muddled undone, but it is a bit more complicated than undoing wool, isn't it? But when they first come here they find it quite panicky, but when they have been here a while they find it all right, like I did.

And the staff try to help to get things better and some staff find it difficult, that's students like D, but she wanted to do the same sort of jobs but she found it difficult.

Sometimes the children find the staff difficult, like when they won't do what they want. Sometimes their mum and dad find it difficult to keep them and look after them. We come to Mrs D to talk about things, and then we find it more easier to understand.

Sometimes they find it frightening at the Bush, and then they get used to it. It's important this – they come to understand about things that go wrong with them at the Bush, and then they get an easier life wherever they go.

But some children find it hard to understand. And when they are at the Bush they find it easier to come to understand about their own lives, isn't that true? – really this is a lot of knowledge isn't it?

Some people go to homes and find the difficulty more complicated, what I mean by that is that the home makes it even more difficult, and they have to go to another home.

Grown-ups come and see first whether they can manage this work, because they have to understand everything about helping children, all that they have to know about that goes on.

People that leave the Bush who found it too hard, find the work they can do – the kind they like best. When they stay it means they've found the sort of work they can do best, and they do all sorts of things to help the children, so that when they leave they find it more easier to get on with other people.

Sometimes grown-ups think of plans that they can do (like having sum cards so that children can get on with their work). At the Bush they can let you start all over again in all sorts of ways. In other schools they wouldn't.

The Bush stops you when you're growing up not knowing all about complicated things from grown-ups not understanding. I'm making up – thinking about the things I really know. This kind of work may need to go on for a long time because when muddled children have children *they* may need this work to be done for them.

I got left behind, and now I'd learn and not get left behind. Because the easier you find things the less panics, and you're not feeling sad all the time, cos then you can't do things and learn all that. But when you are grown-up you don't feel so sad because you know your mother can't live for ever and ever, but when you're a child it's different, and you haven't had your life. But when I get old my life will end, it'll be all a life, that's the sort of thing you need to understand.

It doesn't take very long these days to help people, like it used to be, cos these days people are a bit more clever and have learnt more. [*Aside* DAVID: Why does it feel warmer in your room than in any other room? MYSELF: Is it, perhaps, just because you feel safe in it?]

In the old days they didn't need much help, they didn't have to think so much because they had not learnt so much, so things were not so complicated.

Now people don't have to work so hard, they have stoves instead of fires. In the olden days if a tooth came out they didn't go to a dentist because there wasn't one. They were too busy to be so worried.

They didn't live so long or have so much money, so things are easier now: but people find it a hard world and get into a lot of muddles because everything is so fast. In those days you see people couldn't get run over because there wasn't any cars! (That's a sort of a joke.)

Sometimes people find it hard to keep children because they have to work – that's why children have to go to homes. I mean the parents get into difficulties with their children, and the fathers find it hard to cope with the mothers, and the mothers with the fathers, and the children sometimes find it easier to be somewhere else. [*Aside* DAVID: Poochie is getting much bigger, isn't she? MYSELF: I think you know that Poochie is going to have puppies soon.]

Some people just think about it, some people talk about it and get all the feelings over, that's why talking in talks about feelings makes them understand more.

My essay is different from Mrs D's, and it is the same way about the Bush except that some other people don't think the same thing, do they? It didn't take me long to understand, but it takes other people longer sometimes because they have reasons that make it more difficult to understand. And children at the Bush are not easy to live with, are they?

This is an important thing (my essay being inside Mrs D's) because when you are inside an essay it's more complicated than being inside your mother.

It isn't all that different because it's about the same home – or school. People should really have their own essays about their life.

When you are first a little baby it isn't so hard for your mother to look after you, but as you get bigger it gets difficulter, and the more people you have the harder it would be, and that's an important reason for schools like the Bush, and that means when you've been here and grown older it's easier for your mum to look after you.

There are many interesting points in David's essay, but what I want you to notice especially is the fact that, although the essay is essentially a work of ideas, of rather surprisingly definite conceptualization, nevertheless, without this ever having been stated, David feels that for his little essay to be inside my big one is comparable to a baby being in its mother. This was what I hoped he would feel, and the two asides show how aware he was becoming of his symbolic experience before he made the statement, 'when you are inside an essay it is more complicated than being inside your mother'. The asides showing his growing awareness of what this experience was meaning to him were, you may remember,

David: Why does it feel warmer in your room than in any other room?
Myself: Is it perhaps just because you feel safe in it?'
David: Poochie is getting much bigger, isn't she?

Myself: I think you know that Poochie is going to have puppies soon.

What I was trying to do (and this attempt was successful, as it happened) was to show David that he could actually have symbolic experience with me which could feel real, that he could realize this and store the experience. The experience I offered him had to do with his ideas but, nevertheless, helped him towards symbolization. He had told me that he would never be able to be inside his mother again, any more than he could be inside me, because this would be practically impossible, but here he was being able to find out for himself that in a symbolic way this could be done, and could feel real to him. Of course I had made no interpretation to him. Had I said 'Perhaps to have your essay inside mine would feel like being a baby again inside your mother', I would have made it impossible for him to have the experience; he would just have had another idea for his encyclopedia, as it were.

Sechehaye (1951) calls this 'symbolic realization', and my impression is that when this kind of thing happens the process is symbolic experience followed by realization.

David's essay is full of insight and is especially valuable because less than a year ago David was a very ill child, who behaved as though he were mad. Both his parents are deeply troubled people. David said earlier, 'My mum is always getting into a muddle and so am I.' These 'muddles' were terrible panics which overwhelmed him every few minutes, and made him violent and destructive. Recently he stated, 'I don't get into muddles any more, though I sometimes have a muddle in me – but that's different.' Of course David might not have used the material offered him. Had he not done so, I would have assumed that I was wrong in supposing that he could use these particular symbols to record his experience of having felt contained by me in the treatment situation. As it was, he now had a means of storing both the therapeutic experiences with me and the original experience with his mother, which he knew about intellectually without having reached realization or symbolization. I could, however, only offer him the symbols; it was for David to decide whether he would make use of them.

Michael was just about to settle down for the night, when he suddenly asked me, 'Can you give me something to take into my sleep with me?' I had absolutely nothing appropriate with me, yet I was so sure that he really needed *something*, and that he would know how 'to take it into his sleep with him', that I felt in my coat pocket and found a minute gold safety pin, which I handed to him in a matter of fact sort of way, before saying 'goodnight'.

He accepted the little safety pin, and in the morning came to tell me about a dream – the first dream he could remember.

I dreamt that I was walking along a road. There was a baby with its nappy undone, and it was crying: so I pinned up the nappy with my little gold pin and the baby was all right.

I went on down the road and I met a boy whose braces had broken, so that his trousers were coming down, so I fixed his braces with my little gold pin and the boy was all right.

I went on down the road and I met a man. The wind was blowing cold and the top button had come off his coat, so I gave him my little gold pin to fasten it, and the man was all right.

This was a very important first dream, but all I want to say here is that children can make use of symbols in an astonishing way. I think you will be well aware from what I have said that one of the most important and difficult tasks in working with deeply disturbed children is to establish such means of communication as I have described – so often they have kept some small but precious store of symbols representing their earliest experiences but there has been nobody to whom they felt that they could communicate.

Johnnie, aged seven, whom I met for the first time yesterday, said, 'I am going to sing you a song that has been inside me for a long time.' Here is

JOHNNIE'S SONG
The little boat sails
On the water
And the little boat sails
On the waves.
And the little boat did
And the waves was dead.

> Then the waves had nothing
> To do with the little boat.
> There was nothing for the little boat.

Johnnie's song referred to his babyhood. He talked to me presently about the storm which had caused the waves that tossed the little boat about, until even they were dead and there was nothing left. What we reached later in the session was that there was a time when the little boat was rocking gently on the still and sunlit sea – the time before the storm. As Johnnie said, 'I did not know there was a beginning to the song; it is like there being an o before there is 1.'

I think all of us have unsung songs; unpainted pictures; unwritten pieces of music inside us – the artists, and the poets, and the musicians can communicate these in such a way that they sing, paint or play their earliest experiences, and find a response in us because we have also had a golden age at the beginning of our lives. But the disturbed children whom we try to help in our school all too often have no unsung song within them. They have had nothing about which to sing.

Summary
Symbolization is a necessary process for the internalization and preservation of experience at the beginning of life. I have said very little about the origins of the symbols themselves. On what are symbols based? I think we can only suppose that they have their origins in the earliest bodily experiences and that it is the realization and symbolization of these which provide the prototype for this important process.

In working with emotionally deprived children who have gaps in their primary experience, it becomes essential – having provided missing experience in a way which feels real to the child – that we should help him to realize and symbolize these experiences, so that they can become part of himself and he can reach ideas about the experiences. Such provision of missing experience is often in itself symbolic, but will need to be realized and symbolized all the same if it is to be of value. Children who have succeeded in symbolizing some areas at least of their earliest experience can communicate this to us; it is essential that we should be able to receive and respond to such communications. Children who are able to communicate in this symbolic way will be able to tell us all sorts of 'inside' things about themselves, and their own inner worlds, which would otherwise not be reached.

Lastly, conceptualization is no substitute for original experience. This is a process of emotional evolution of individual personality, not an organization of fixed ideas about child rearing.

Chapter 12

Id sublimation?

I have looked everywhere for references related to the notions and ideas in this chapter. Whether they exist or not, I have not, in fact, been able to find many.

My first reference, which I came across twenty years ago, is from Freud, from his wonderful 'Leonardo da Vinci and a memory of his childhood'.

> In reality Leonardo was not devoid of passion: he did not lack the divine spark which is directly or indirectly the driving force – *il primo motore* – behind all human activity. He had merely converted his passion into a thirst for knowledge; he then applied himself to investigation with the persistence, constancy, and penetration which is derived from passion, and at the climax of intellectual labour, when knowledge had been won, he allowed the long restrained affect to break loose and to flow away freely, as a stream of water drawn from a river is allowed to flow away when its work is done. [I cannot think of this process as being an example of ego-mediate sublimation.] And finally the *instinct*, which had become overwhelming, swept him away until the connection with the demands of his art was severed.
>
> (Freud, 1910, pp. 74–6)

Our psycho-analytic studies of neurotic people have however led us to form two further expectations which it would be gratifying to find in each particular case. We consider it probable that an instinct like this is of excessive strength was already active in the subject's earliest childhood, and that its supremacy was estab-lished by impressions in the child's life . . . The sexual instinct is particularly well fitted to make contributions of this kind *since it is endowed with a capacity for sublimation.*

(Freud, 1910, pp. 77–8, my italics)

And another passage:

In virtue of a special disposition, the third type which is the rarest and most perfect, escapes both inhibition of thought and neurotic compulsive thinking. It is true that here too sexual repression comes about, but it does not succeed in relegating a component instinct of sexual desire to the unconscious. Instead, the libido evades the fate of repression by being sublimated from the very beginning . . . (sublimation instead of an irruption from the unconscious).

(Freud, 1910, p. 80)

At the end of this fascinating study Freud wrote: 'We are obliged to look for the source of the tendency to repression and the capacity for sublimation in the organic foundations of character on which the mental structure is only afterwards erected' (Freud, 1910, p. 136).

Poincaré (1908) writes: 'In the subliminal self, on the contrary, reigns what I should call liberty, if we might give that name to the simple absence of discipline and to the disorder born of chance. Only the disorder itself permits unexpected combinations.' This is the part of the mind through which I think the id can achieve sublimation – through sudden inspiration or the breakthrough of unconscious thought into flashes of insight (I believe in a process of unconscious thought).

The material which follows was given to me by Sue Treloar, who is the 'therapeutic resource' (see Chapter 7) of the Cottage group in the Cotswold Community, where I work as a consultant.

Whilst the Cottage group were away on holiday in Devon this year, it was decided to keep a scrapbook of photographs and accounts of what happened each day. The boys were also encouraged to draw pictures of activities and of scenes they had enjoyed, yet during the day the suggestion met with little response. However, at suppertime there was suddenly an enthusiasm and delight for drawing pictures. As the week progressed this time of day became very important to the group. One of the grown-ups would read a story, while another grown-up would serve out the supper. Thus, curled up in chairs and wrapped in blankets, many of the boys took up the pencils and paper that were there and produced some wonderful pictures. Tom, who had never drawn anything but an occasional picture of a house, drawn completely with ruled lines and with no colour, produced a picture of a flowering tree, using the crayons to make the page a mass of life and colour. Michael, who rarely drew anything at all, produced a number of pictures of large and colourful crabs, some on the shore and some at the bottom of the sea, whilst Sam created a landscape picture showing the patchwork of fields so typical of Devon, each coloured in to represent the different crops growing there. There was so much pleasure gained from this time of day when the boys could be warm, receive food and a story and draw some wonderful pictures, it remained a special memory of the holiday.

The Cottage group is made up of the most unintegrated boys in the Cotswold Community, who are, in a symbolic way, getting back to 'the point of failure' as Winnicott called it. These deeply disturbed boys were warm, happy, well fed and cared for. They had pencils and colour and paper, and with this they sublimated their instinctive, primary bliss into remarkable pictures – dream pictures. They had very little ego, if one thinks of the ego being made from experience. They have had hardly any early experience, but they have enormous amounts of id and harsh super-egos. In this situation they found inspiration at a very early level, which enabled them to sublimate the id.

Perhaps I am suggesting that there could be an id ideal? This would explain certain kinds of creativity.

Freud wrote: 'Reflection at once shows us that no vicissitudes can be experienced or undergone by the id, except by way of the ego, which is the representative of the outer world to the id. Nevertheless, it is not possible to speak of direct inheritance by the ego . . .'

Do we believe this? What if there is little or no ego? May not id reach sublimation without ego?

Chapter 13

Secondary deprivation – infant- and primary-school age

I am considering the possible concept of a secondary deprivation which would take place at infant and primary-school age. We have focused our thoughts concerning deprivation on the first years of life, and may have not realized that circumstances can produce a later and very disastrous form of deprivation.

Babies can be deprived only in a fairly obvious manner, that is to say, by the failure of the mother to become preoccupied with the baby or by the actual absence of the mother or mother figure. The later deprivation which I am considering is the result of children being pushed into premature independence. For example, once a child can *go* to bed he may no longer be *put* to bed. Once he is able to feed himself he is unlikely to be fed; the holding and containing quality of maternal care may deteriorate in a way which is disastrous. Children may be left to look after themselves before they are really ready to do so.

This sort of management leads to further harm, for example, there may cease to be a regular bedtime or mealtimes. There may be no structure in regard to television. I have seen a child of six left to prepare his own sandwiches for school, to cook his own meals and so on. This state of affairs leads to a very deep resentment in children, a feeling of rejection, not realized by the mothers, who are often working, or in other ways demanding a life of their own.

Children who grow up in this fashion become rebellious, angry and anti-social. I believe that this is a deep root of riot and violence, which can be altered only by a change in the attitude of many parents. In the same way children should not *have* to leave home at sixteen years of age. They may be ready and willing to do so, but there are many youngsters who need a longer period at home. (Of course there are thousands of children who are cared for in a very different way, so that the ebb and flow of growth can take place, and their needs can be met as long as they are present.) I have seen a boy of twelve years old having weeks of sleepless nights after having seen video nasties *at home*. There are programmes on television and articles and pictures in newspapers which may be quite unsuitable for a young child and may have a deep effect upon him. In the same way such children should not be left to roam the streets – many awful incidents would not happen if children were kept more at home.

My proposal is that there should be groups of mothers, led by trained psychotherapists or by trained and experienced social workers, meeting weekly, over a considerable period, giving help and advice in solving problems of management – not therapeutic groups, but with a therapeutic aim, rather than educational.

For example, we find at the Cotswold Community that children love to cook and to be involved in cookery situations. There is a tremendous difference between a potato baked in the oven and a bag of chips. I believe that the fury and frenzy which is to be seen among young people – black and white – arise from this kind of deprivation and the consequent dependence on excitement rather than contentment. Of course there are all too many children who have been severely deprived at a primary stage and who may never recover without treatment. These are the frozen delinquents who tend to lead gangs in inner-city riots or on football fields.

The groups which I have in mind would be set up within the community. The mothers themselves would meet during the day, once weekly. A group would consist of eight mothers who feel a need for discussion about difficulties with regard to primary-school-age children. There would be an informal link with the schools concerned and referral to clinics where this was needed.

Parents, both fathers and mothers, tend to expect their children to be grown up and independent before they are ready to take so much responsibility; structure, control and above all caring are needed in many cases.

Chapter 14

Interpretation outside psychoanalysis

I assumed until recently that interpretation belonged strictly to the fields of psychoanalysis and psychotherapy. However, in view of the work in which I have been involved as a consultant psychotherapist at the Cotswold Community, I have broadened my views, and feel that interpretation can be used naturally and individually in other fields. This does not mean that interpretation can ever be employed without care and thought, but I am certain that it is actually used in other ways, and can be as valuable or, alas, as dangerous as when it is an analytic technique.

The workers/therapists at the Cotswold Community are, for the most part, young graduates who are often social workers. They have lively, enquiring minds and are deeply concerned with the delinquent adolescents whom they are trying to help – often with considerable success.

The theories on which the therapy in the Cotswold Community is based are those of D.W. Winnicott, and turn on the vital concept of integration of the individual and the disastrous results of failure to integrate due to early and severe deprivation. Usually the boys come to us in a quite unintegrated state, and often unused to symbolization, due to lack of primary experience and of the 'realization' which that brings about.

The young people who help them often themselves have one or two sessions of analysis each week; all belong to training groups in the Cotswold Community, run by senior, often analysed Community workers. I have a session with each of four households every week and see a considerable number of individuals – heads of houses and people who come to me on a 'demand basis' organized by John Whitwell (the Principal of the Community). We have an adequate library, and everyone reads – usually in their spare time.

I also see each week what are termed the therapeutic resource people who are responsible for therapy in the household teams and who give supervision and support to all the members of a household. These therapeutic resource people are well read, have nearly all had some analysis and organize reporting (Context Profiles and Need Assessments – described in Chapter 22) in their particular household. They are selected with great care and are remarkable people.

Communication is regarded as the main form of therapy, other than concern and reliability. Each boy meets his particular therapist alone, for one or more short periods each week, during which time communication at every sort of level takes place between boy and therapist. It is during these meeting times that interpretation is used in a natural way, usually appearing in the form of a response to a symbolic communication. For example, a boy talking in a symbolic way about the deep anger and despair which he is unable to express in any direct way plays a game which I invented a long time ago, in which the boy is given three sheets of paper, numbered 1, 2 and 3. He is asked to tell a story in three pictures – a beginning, a middle and an end. The therapist must then try to guess the context of the story. This is nearly always possible, but, if the therapist makes mistakes, the boy is delighted to correct him. At no point is there a direct interpretation, but within the symbolic contents of the story comments can be made of a kind valuable to the boy.

So, in one such story, the boy draws an angry dog in a locked garden, with a newspaper in his mouth. (There is much information about the boy, withheld from his father.) The interpretation in this case was a suggestion that a newspaper boy (the main character) could give the dog a biscuit (good experience), thereby freeing the newspaper to be read by the man in the second picture (so the father can learn about the boy's feelings).

Some boys prefer to play with a bag full of small objects; they can then talk about their play, and it can be discussed in the same way. We also use Winnicott's squiggle game, when the boy makes a squiggle with a pencil, which he then talks about with the therapist – the squiggle can reveal a great deal. I remember such a squiggle which again and again turned into a boat at sea. Nothing that the boy or I could say was of any use until I happened, one day, to ask him where he himself was situated in the squiggle. It turned out that he was in the harbour on the quay, beyond which was a town which contained all sorts of valuable things – people, houses, animals. The squiggle was in fact a view from the harbour out to sea, where the boat floated. In all such work the therapist uses only the symbols in the story, which when discussed in an appropriate way, can reveal much of the boy's inner reality.

These boys may be tough, fifteen-year-old delinquents, but they do not seem to inhibit in any way, except in rare cases of extreme resistance. Through the provision of primary experience and subsequent realization, boys begin to communicate, making use of the kind of material which I have described – never suggested to them by the therapist. Gradually they become able to describe their despair and the awfulness of this deprivation.

One boy spoke to me of finding himself in an icy waste, with high mountains all round him and no hope of escape. Eventually we were able to find a way out of this dreadful place, and he found fields and woods.

Symbolization is the only way in which these deprived young-sters can communicate their desperate feelings, and if we can understand and make good use of the symbols we can bring them relief and understanding, which makes acting out no longer necessary. This technique of symbolic communication I have developed with others over the years and find invaluable in helping workers to interpret deeply disturbed and deprived children.

Chapter 15

Panic

I have been very concerned with the treatment of 'panic' states, described by Winnicott as states of 'unthinkable anxiety'. Over the years I have had several patients referred to me by Winnicott in whom the main symptom was panic. We discussed the phenomenon on many occasions and were able to treat the devastating symptoms of this disorder. However, we were not able to be exact in statements about 'unthinkable anxiety'. I remember Winnicott saying that the most important factor in the treatment of panic is the acceptance of its reality.

Panic is often described as 'hyperventilation', which certainly describes the acute over-breathing which is one of the major symptoms of panic. However, Winnicott's 'unthinkable anxiety' seems to me to present a much more complex picture of the phenomenon.

At the Cotswold Community, where we try to help delinquent, disturbed young people, we constantly find that panic is one of the main features of their personalities. These panics are extremely violent and overwhelming, they can have a close connection with murderous and violent attacks on adults and their treatment presents great problems.

Since before I came to work in the Community – seventeen years ago – the treatment has been to hold the panicking boy, of course in a way that is not involving any pain for the boy, and with steady and continued communication of an explanatory kind. However, I have never been happy about this approach nor have I ever used this technique myself, but, since my own method has been through communication of an intuitive kind, I have been in no position to suggest any better approach.

However, recently, I have had a short experience of panic

myself, which seems to me to be a better position from which to discuss the problem. Apparently it turns up in 10 per cent of the population, and I suspect in practically anyone for a few minutes at a time. I had a sudden attack of panic one afternoon, without any warning or explanation. I knew what I was suffering from, so I decided to try and understand the panic state and, if possible, deal with it as I had helped my patients to do. (I should make clear that I did not have severe panic states, they did not last long, they were contained and did not affect my functioning.)

I came to the conclusion that if I was feeling unthinkable anxiety this might have some root. I decided that this root must be found in some thinkable objective anxiety which had been prolonged and finally changed into panic. I found that this idea made sense. I had been anxious for some time in an objective way about my husband's health. This anxiety lasted for quite a time and turned into panic when my anxiety was confirmed and became too acute for me to bear. (Since then my husband has had treatment and completely recovered.) As soon as I became clear about this fact, I had fewer and less drastic panics and these have gradually ceased.

Thinking of the boys at the Cotswold Community, I found myself considering the problem of a small boy assaulted by a violent adult. Of course, after the first occasion such a child would feel acute anxiety and dread that the experience might be repeated. However, when such a trauma occurred constantly, this anxiety would change into severe panic states, such as we have seen in our experiences.

With treatment the panics are gradually reduced and disappear. However, in the secondary stage of treatment, following a deep dependent relationship with a therapist, the boy seems to reach the earlier objective anxiety for himself and reports this to the therapist. I hope that, if these ideas are confirmed, children will not need to be 'held' in a panic, except perhaps on the first occasion, when the therapist would explain to the boy the nature of his panic and the possibility of treatment through realization, rather like abreaction in the treatment of trauma.

I hope that if my findings are found to be valid, we should start to think of the treatment of panic in a different and perhaps more therapeutic way.

Chapter 16

Holding

The management of violence in the course of treating deprived and unintegrated adolescents presents great problems. The presenting symptom is usually panic, which can explode without any warning, causing infinite damage to people and things. The best solution of all is anticipation, but often the panic happens so suddenly that this is not possible. Nevertheless, if one has any reason to suppose that a boy is likely to panic, the worker will be well advised to discuss this with the boy, including the measures which will be taken to contain the violence which so often goes with panic. Holding combined with communication are the techniques which we use in the Cotswold Community – but we never use holding unless really necessary and that can only be judged from experience.

The boy may throw himself at the adult, on the floor or on a bed or chair. If a boy is on the floor the best plan is to kneel by his side, holding his shoulders and his hands and keeping clear of his feet, which may be kicking. Sometimes it is possible – on a bed or chair for example – to put one's arm around the boy's shoulders, with the other hand holding his hands. The boy must never be hurt by anything which the worker does to control him, but may hurt himself in his struggles. It is essential to talk to him in a quiet voice throughout the whole experience, emphasizing that he will soon be better, that the worker understands that the boy cannot help what he is doing – that he is in a state of anxiety beyond fear and that one day he will not have to panic any more, as we come to understand him.

Sometimes the boy only screams or swears, but at other times, especially if he knows the worker well, he will answer, and may indeed say very important things which give clues to the origin of the panic. What is certain is that the boy both hears and remembers what the adult has said to him, however out of touch he may seem to be.

It is easy to tell when the panic is over; the boy relaxes, asks for a drink or food and may go to sleep. Other boys may interfere, either to help or hinder, particularly new boys who may feel that the panicking boy is being ill treated. This makes it important for all boys to be told about panic and control.

The real risk in the question of holding is that the holder may become angry, or at least impatient. It is important to understand that the boy will recognize the anger or impatience. The holder may have already been hit and, while he does the right things, he may be furious inside himself, revengeful, and the holding may become retaliation. It is essential that the holder has the right feelings – compassion, empathy and some grasp of the terrible experiences the boy must have been through to reach this condition. Sometimes it is well worth while saying so: 'Something awful happened to you that you do not actually remember'; 'A long time ago, someone terrified you into panic.'

What do battered babies feel? They do not consciously remember, but they are still suffering from the trauma. It is important to remember that there is unconscious memory to be considered and that this has lasting effects, despite the mechanism of repression.

What we have to do is to make some sort of reparation for the trauma – gentle, concerned and compassionate handling, and yet sufficiently strong to protect the child, oneself and others.

One of the chief difficulties is that the child may have no idea why he is panicking. Eventually he may reach realization, with our help, and then he will not need to be held any more – that is to say, he will understand the source and cause of panic. If possible it should be another grown-up who does the holding, rather than the adult who has been attacked by the boy.

The danger in this technique lies in the fact that adults can get angry, revengeful and violent, without realizing that this has happened. This means that there must be strict monitoring on holding: the head of the household and the therapeutic resource must be very clear that the holding is really necessary and carried out in an appropriate, concerned way. I think that any instance of holding should be reported and considered. Nothing *said* by a boy should be a cause for holding nor should a boy be held for a moment longer than is actually necessary.

All in all I do not like the practice of holding, but I do not see what other solution presents itself in the difficult situation of a violent panic in a deprived adolescent. Nobody who has been in the Community for less than six months should hold a boy. In some places a boy is locked up in isolation; in one community several adults used to hold down a panicking boy. Certainly other boys are greatly disturbed by seeing a grown-up attacked without any effort being made to control the attacker, but I am sure that no boy should ever be isolated or roughly handled in a retaliatory manner and that holding should be a last resource, rarely used.

Chapter 17

The management of violence

This paper is a study of everyday violence in the individual and of how this can be managed in a residential place. Extreme violence – murder or a murderous attack – is rare, and when it takes place makes certain steps necessary (for example, the instant removal of the violent person to somewhere totally containing and secure). I have not considered group violence in this paper either, because this subject needs to be thought about in its own right.

Violence, together with the problems of aggressive children, is such a vast subject that I judged it best to select a particular sphere.

Essentially, the management of violence is concerned with the question of responsibility. A violent act is committed, and people ask, 'But why?' They seek for reasons in the history of the violent person by categorizing emotional disorder and in flaws of the environment; usually the reasons they find are 'out there', rather than 'in here'.

The mother of a patient said to me recently, 'Jane is quite unmanageable. We had a terrible day – she has ruined our family life with her violence.' When I asked in some detail about this day in Jane's life, I found that she had been persecuted, frustrated and deprived by her parents and the rest of her family. Furthermore, her mother told me about a series of episodes which all reflected very badly on herself and Jane's family, without noticing that this was so, that Jane's reactions were the inevitable result of intolerable stress. We are accustomed to allow for a large measure of projection in our patients' descriptions of family encounters, but here was the mother speaking, without guilt and without insight, telling me in all good faith about her child's violence.

And now here am I talking about something 'out there' because it is easier to think about parents of violent children than about ourselves trying to help these same children and sometimes behaving with as little guilt and as little insight as the mother I have described. Let us try to tolerate looking 'in here' at our own responsibility for violence.

One could start by saying that the management of violence is its prevention. By this statement, I mean that, since all acting out is a breakdown in communication, it is our responsibility to keep in communication with the children in our care. Jane's family was not in touch with her – there was no common language in which feelings could be expressed in words, so the feelings bypassed communication and erupted as physical violence.

In order to understand the therapeutic value of invariable response to all communication from children of any age, it is important to grasp the concept of 'the spontaneous gesture' (Winnicott). The baby smiles at the mother and reaches out to her: the mother's response is an essential to the baby's emotional well-being. If the mother does not or cannot (because of her own defences) respond to the spontaneous gesture, then the baby is reaching out as though for ever into infinity. Eventually in such a case the baby ceases to attempt those gestures, having reached despair. Our response to what a deprived child tries to communicate may re-establish his belief in the possibility of response to his reaching out. Recently a child aged ten called Timothy drew for me a picture of himself in his cot as a baby: the picture showed him lying flat in the cot with one hand showing between the bars. He said, 'That's me trying to reach my mum – it's a bit like a cage, the cot, isn't it?' I replied that this was so, but that perhaps the bars of this cage which kept his mother away from him but were also the bars of *her* cage: in other words, her defences, protecting him from her violence, but also isolating him.

We have to be careful that children find *us* when they reach out, and that they do not again find defences instead of people. A boy at the Cotswold Community said to me, 'It's different here from other places.' I asked what was the greatest difference, to which he answered, 'People really listen to you – they don't just hear you – they *listen* – nobody has ever listened to me like that before.'

Sometimes people are afraid of what children will say, of the dreadful unanswerable questions they may ask. This is a valid fear, but it is also valid to say that just listening is therapy. At first much of what our clients say will be paranoid accusations and complaints against all who are in authority of any kind. We can listen to such complaints that are without logical reasoning, accepting the reality of the feelings expressed and leaving the objective reality alone for the present. Gradually the child will start to communicate his dread and his helplessness.

During the last few years at the Cotswold Community we have become accustomed to looking into the face of violence, searching for the breakdown in communication on our part which has driven a boy into committing a violent act. The astonishing fact is that we have usually – because of the honesty of the workers – been able to find the point of breakdown. I shall be saying more about these discoveries presently, but first I want to draw your attention to the effect which this sort of realization has upon workers in a place.

Hitherto, there had always been anxiety and worry in regard to violent action, especially if it happened outside the community – worry for the boy and for the reputation of the place in society outside. This was, however, an 'out there' kind of anxiety, leading to a lot of discussion about the boy's case history, his curent situation in the community and at home, his abnormal EEG and so on. Nowadays, of course, these are still all to be considered, but there are also the questions: 'What hasn't been talked about?' 'Where have we failed him?' 'Is this our fault?' *This* sort of anxiety is 'in here' – immediate, urgent and very disturbing. I do not believe that we should avoid this worry, which is why I think of violence in connection with our own personal and professional sense of responsibility. Once we are looking at violence from this 'in here' point of view, we add a dimension to our perception of an event which may not only show us where we have failed *this time*, but which may also help us to perceive the need for communication *next time* and thereby to anticipate a violent outburst.

Nobody except Jane seemed to be violent in her family constellation. Actually, there was plenty of hidden violence, especially between her parents, who, although they never had 'rows', used Jane as a vehicle for their secret rages with each other – Jane acted out their fury. When, ultimately, she made a recovery, the hidden violence in both her parents and her siblings could suddenly be seen more clearly in their relationships with each other, because Jane no longer accepted a safety valve/scapegoat role for her family.

Sometimes in residential work one meets workers who always seem to be calm, kind people, but around whom violence seems to flourish in the children in their care. This is the same phenomenon – the children are acting out for the worker, just as Jane acted out for her family. Deprived children will expect us to behave like their parents; it is an awful thought that (however unconsciously) we may fulfil these expectations. I say 'unconsciously', but, after all, the unconscious is part of the person, for which one must ultimately accept responsibility.

People working with deprived children have to learn a lot of painful things about themselves, if they are to be of use to children: for example, to become aware of the violence in themselves. It is not in question that there will be violent feelings in anybody, but the questions remain. Firstly, does the person know about these feelings? And secondly, how does he or she contain them? I have sometimes said to staff at the Cotswold Community and the Mulberry Bush that I feel that workers in such places go through something a bit like an analysis – without an analyst, sessions, a couch *or* a fee! – but with a lot of pain. Their work and their personal lives become enriched through this experience, and they improve their emotional economy, but the gaining of insight must always be a slow and painful process.

I have said that there must not be a breakdown in communication between adults and children if violence is to be contained. There cannot, however, be a breakdown in something which has never been set up. Communication of the kind I mean does not exist in any planned form in a hierarchical institution. At the Mulberry Bush, where planned open communication has been in action for quite a long time, there is practically no violence or acting out of any kind (stealing or window-breaking are rare occurrences). The police have told us that they are impressed by the small amount of acting out in the neighbourhood by the Cotswold Community boys. In both places, children and adolescents have opportunities each day for both group and individual talking with a grown-up (of course I am speaking of 'open' communication, grown-ups talking not *to* children but *with* them).

One of the areas where a breakdown in communication can easily lead to violence is the use of television. Often children watch 'telly' while grown-ups get work done. This may mean – will mean – that they sometimes will see disturbing things on the screen which they may not be able to discuss with grown-ups. In my view, there must always be an adult watching with the children and prepared to talk about the programme with them at the time and immediately afterwards. Recently there were pictures on the news of striking prisoners on the roofs of prisons. Boys at the Cotswold Community who saw these scenes climbed on to the roofs next day and threatened a similar strike. They had seen the news pictures alone, so that no grown-up had a chance to intervene in their projective identification with the prisoners or had realized that this had taken place.

Having accepted our share of responsibility for violent actions we must ask what the child's share of personal responsibility for violent behaviour is. Roughly one can equate degree of responsibility with degree of integration as an individual reached by the person who has committed the violent act. Unintegrated people of any age are unable to contain conflict, to make a choice, to feel personal guilt or compassion for others or to accept responsibility.

At the beginning of life, the baby and the mother form what Margaret Little has called a primary unity. During the first year there is a slow and continuous process in which the baby gradually separates out from the mother and becomes a person in his own right. Essentially, one can say that he moves from being *contained* (by the mother) to becoming a container (able to contain personal guilt and anxiety). Emotionally deprived children are those who have not completed this process, which depends on the provision of primary experience by the mother or mother substitute. The self is built from such experiences so that where there are gaps in primary experience, there will be corresponding gaps in the self.

The populations of residential nurseries, children's homes,

schools for the maladjusted and approved schools are made up in nearly all cases of a mixture of integrated and unintegrated children. It is essential that the needs of all deprived children should be met, and it must be clearly understood that the nature of these needs depends on degree of integration. So far, it is usual for the behaviour of unintegrated children to be recognized as 'different' from that of others, and for them to be labelled behaviour disordered, character disordered, psychopathic personalities and so on. These labels – technical or otherwise – emphasize the difference between these children and others, while totally failing to suggest that (although they cannot benefit from what is available in the way of management) they are in need of special treatment. This need is so much less easy to recognize, for many reasons, in unintegrated children than in integrated, functioning children, especially because of the breakdown of communication into acting out.

The therapist working with integrated children depends on transference phenomena and on verbal interpretation within the strict limits of the therapeutic hour. The therapist working with unintegrated children must depend on personal involvement, on symbolic actions (adaptations) and on establishing communication in place of acting out.

In the Cotswold Community it has been possible to classify the approved-school children by assessment of integration into the four house groups. This kind of assessment is not usually available in referral reports, but I have found that residential staff are quite able to carry out this sort of in-living diagnosis themselves, in consultation with me. We have used two factors only in assessing degree of integration: these have been panic and disruption. Where both these factors are present we assume unintegration. Both phenomena are easy to recognize, once their nature is understood. Panic is often described as temper tantrum, disruption, as anti-social behaviour. *Panic*, rarely mentioned in psychiatric reports, is the hallmark of unintegration and represents traumatic – unthinkable – experience at an early age. It produces claustrophobia and agoraphobia, states of disorientation and a total loss of any sense of identity: the victim falls to pieces in a state beyond terror. He may be totally immobilized or, more frequently, he may hit out, scream, destroy things or attack other people. *Disruption,* described by Erikson as play disruption, can be seen in action very easily. The child comes into a situation where others are functioning, either in work or play, and at once compulsively breaks into the group and breaks up the activity. Panic and disruption are familiar to any experienced worker, but may not have been seen as signals of distress.

Most violence – apart from single isolated acts – springs from these unintegrated people, whether they are in residential nurseries or in prisons. Winnicott describes unintegrated children in treatment:

> In Hostels B and C, where children lie about on the floor, cannot get up, refuse to eat, mess their pants, steal whenever they feel a loving impulse, torture cats, kill mice and bury them so as to have a cemetery where they can go and cry, in these hostels there should be a notice: visitors not admitted. The wardens of these hostels have the perpetual job of covering naked souls, and they see as much suffering as can be seen in a mental hospital for adults. How difficult it is to keep a good staff under these conditions!

The acceptance of responsibility implies the presence of a functioning ego, which is absent in these children. We have to supply the functioning ego ourselves, and to contain and *hold the violence and the child* together. A small boy at the Bush, speaking of the worker on whom he was becoming deeply dependent, said, 'You see Desmond can hold on to me *and* my temper.'

If integrated people break down into violence, we can assume that they have for that moment disintegrated: a breakdown into disintegration is *not* the same phenomenon as a state of unintegration (in which integration remains so far unknown). Integrated neurotic children and young people should be helped to contain and communicate their violent feelings and should be expected to do so. Unintegrated ones cannot contain violent feelings – or for that matter anything else. By helping them to communicate, by *listening* and responding in an appropriate way, we may enable them to contain their feelings by transposing them into the symbols we call words.

Another factor to be carefully considered in regard to violence is what Robert Ardrey has called the 'Territorial Imperative'. He and others have noted the disastrous effects of overcrowding on many types of animal; it would seem that space for individual emotional and physical life is essential to human beings also. It has been found that people crowded together, in prisoner-of-war camps, for example, soon become irritable and then violent. People need living space and some degree of insulation.

This is true of normal integrated individuals, and is even more true of unintegrated people who in any case have no boundaries to themselves, so that boundaries must be provided for them. Deprived children sleeping six to eight in a dormitory, for example, are much more likely to become violent if there are no partitions between each pair of beds. The presence of such low (shoulder-high) partitions in the Mulberry Bush has minimized violence at dangerous moments when tension is high and very small incidents can spark off violence. The unintegrated children settle down well in their specially built containing beds, two children to each bay – insulated but not isolated. The same type of insulation is needed in classrooms in which unintegrated children are to be taught.

So here we have several hazards to be tackled in order to prevent violence:

1 to accept responsibility for keeping lines of communication always open, so that violent acting out can be converted into the communication of anger;
2 to contain and know our violent feelings so that we do not need to use children to act these out for us;
3 to respect the 'territorial imperative' and to provide insulation for children;
4 to be responsible for containing children who are not themselves able to accept responsibility.

We come now to violence which we have not been able to prevent. Richard Balbernie, head of the Cotswold Community, describes a violent boy as follows.

At fourteen and a half Bill was admitted to a residential special school. He did not settle at all at first. He found it impossible to accept the slightest disciplinary demand impersonally; each was a calculated personal affront. Then, after a period of six months of testing the limits to extremes, he became increasingly physically violent, unmanageable and abusive. These outbursts were frightening (he was a heavily built, powerful boy) and were provoked by trivial remarks taken by the boy as deadly insults. He attached himself to a staff member and then for a while the general intensity and unpredictable discharge of the tensions and outbursts diminished. Towards one staff member, however, he became increasingly provocative, crude and primitive in behaviour, straining at the relationship unremittingly. Behind the scenes he encouraged and provoked sex play and sexual interference among the younger children and derived some vicarious satisfaction from this, but the satisfaction was derived largely from the complex strains and the reactions it provoked among staff and in staff relationships.

He made no relationships with other children. By the end of the first year he was very violent, unpredictable and abusive with all adults (some of these outbursts were now, in fact, becoming very dangerous). His pilfering concentated on the property and room of the staff member with whom he had developed an intense, dependent, yet still extremely aggressive tie. Any separation (bedtime and settling were significantly especially difficult) was liable to activate intense feelings of anxiety. His obscenities and attitudes made him an isolate among the other boys. He bought his mates through a mixture of tyranny and favour-granting.

Bill became increasingly abusive and dependent, and at the same time desperate in feeling that he was 'not a fit person to have such a friend'. Considerable guilt surrounding the relationship with his father was expressed at this time and the staff member required much support from the remainder of the staff through this period and during the emergence of the underlying and deeply aggressive and primitive elements which erupted into the new and developing interaction. The increasing dependence and decreasing hatred, in fact, created such an element of stress and uncertainty in the relationship with this unlovable boy to the point where the staff member said he felt 'completely demoralized'.

Bill then began to attach himself to another staff member (a social worker) and the pattern was repeated. The intensity was slightly diminished, although adults were continuously played off one against the other as 'good' and 'bad' objects and the remainder of the staff played an important part in the background and outside this drama. The school reports at this stage stress: (1) the boy's inability to respond to ordinary support and affection; (2) the lack of any indications that he might ever build up any loyalties or participate in any constructive way in the life of the group; (3) an increase of seemingly pathological lying and evasiveness; (4) the fact that relationships had to be on an infantile 'on demand' and undemanding basis or else they become stormy, abusive, violent and at the same time ingratiating, sidling and wheedling; (5) there was a tremendous and very painful underlying emotional charge the nature of which was quite split off from consciousness; (6) the boy's punitive attitude to himself; (7) his complete inability to respond to a role in a classroom or in any school organization.

His violence and unpredictability were such that one child on whom his violence suddenly fell jumped out of an upstairs window to escape from him and broke an arm.

The only quiescent periods were at those times when, for a while, all normal social demands could be removed and he could be treated quite individually and differently from anyone else. These were also, however, periods which roused great anxiety and insecurity for him as feeling incurably different, although his special, individual needs in this respect were understood, discussed and accepted by the other children. He became increasingly suspicious, defensive, and also increasingly believed in his own lying. This position became, in fact, of great importance to him – what he believed to be real (and which was real for him, in fact) had to be unquestioningly believed by others if violence was to be averted.

This is a most vivid and clear picture which I am sure you will recognize – we have all met people like Bill. The people in the place who were trying to help him, with skill and devotion, found themselves impoverished and exhausted by the scale of his demands and the force of his violence. Bill left the school before he reached recovery but he was beginning to recover – what I think of as coming backwards through a quickset hedge.

The act of violence itself is *usually* a *panic*, so that the need is to hold the panicker (which sometimes needs the efforts of two people) and to talk to him continuously, regardless of obscenities or spittle, bites, kicks or screams. The talking should be assurance that he will recover from this state, that you are here and so is he; that you know how terrible he is feeling; that this has been happening to him all his life, and so on. *He will hear you. Never should a violent person in a state of panic be left alone* – he will feel this as annihilation. I speak with this degree of assurance because I and others have seen many children through panic states and we have their testimony to the value of the kind of treatment I have described.

The same approach is suitable for a particular type of violence which providentially is fairly rare. Certain apparently integrated children, adolescents and adults have a pocket of violence around which integration has been built. This pocket could be termed psychotic, providing that the term psychotic is used in a special way to mean 'static' – a pocket within the personality so damaged as to be incapable of evolvement. I believe that such a person is not unintegrated but has disintegrated, probably during the second year of life due to traumatic pressure. Although the child may seem to have matured and developed fairly normally, functioning adequately in most fields, there will be this static violent pocket, quite split off from consciousness and capable of exploding into the ultimate of violence at any time (usually triggered off by some association). When this sort of person is in a violent state he must be held and contained and is probably too far out of touch to receive verbal communication. However, after such outbursts – between this one and the next – it is possible gradually to bring the knowledge of the static pocket to the child's consciousness, to explain to him that there may always be this part of himself, capable of doing terrible things, for which he must accept responsibility. Such communication, however, can only be made when the defences – the shell – have been sufficiently strengthened through good experience and the increase of ego functioning to enable the child to contain the dangerous pocket within himself: this is a very difficult process.

When dealing with a violent state in a child, then,

1 we should never leave him alone;
2 we should hold him firmly;
3 we should communicate with him throughout.

We have considered the anticipation of violence, the management of violence in action. Now let us think about violence in retrospect.

Those people who habitually act out in violent ways are those who are not aware of a future, or of a past – they live in an extended present. They may admit or deny an act of violence, but this statement is likely to be merely an intellectual exercise; they do not often *realize* what they have done. As I have said before, unintegrated people do not contain experience. If, however, one is in communication with such a person and therefore in a position to re-establish communication with him following breakdown, what is likely to emerge will be rather different.

It will be useless to try to awaken his guilt or to arouse his compassion for the victim of his violence. What may be of value is to help him piece together the history of the hours leading up to the outbreak. If you can cover the ground with him on several occasions in this way, you and he may find certain common factors in the period just before the violence. Very often there will be an unresolved paranoid position in which the child describes what he feels to have been some gross injustice towards himself (for which the violent act is a revenge) – for example, Tom said to me, 'I had a debt to pay.' It will be important to accept the reality of his *feelings* of persecution, however 'untrue' this may be in objective reality. Do not argue with him, but try to reflect his very real feelings: 'You must have been feeling pretty awful to do such a thing . . .'

There may on such occasions be a series of minor frustrations building up into a crisis for which the panic violence is emotionally a safety valve. Henry said, 'I felt I was going to blow up.' Paul threw his valued bicycle into a pond; nobody could understand what had happened to lead to this action. A skilled worker talking with Paul discovered that the two young men looking after him that day (a holiday period) had faithfully reproduced the attitudes of his rejecting parents. One had nagged at him incessantly (as Paul's mother used to do) and the other had withdrawn from him, become remote and detached (like his father). Of course this was all quite unconscious and there was an element of chance in respect of the moods of the two workers; but nevertheless it was this constellation which precipitated Paul into violence. Paul was able to realize how the workers (whom he liked and trusted) had affected him in this way. Because he began to grasp the dynamics of the situation he was able to bring a little insight into the next comparable situation, and to see resemblances in cycles of events.

Deprived and deeply disturbed children and adolescents have talked to me about their violence. Often they describe its onset as something physical: 'I get cold and shivery, and there is a prickly feeling . . .' Since panic is essentially psychosomatic, this is not surprising. Peter learnt for himself to recognize a physical feeling which was a sign of an impending outburst of violence: 'I'd have to bash this chap if it went on . . . so I got off the bus and I walked a long way . . .'

Sometimes we may be able to connect the present with the distant past, as in Paul's case when he re-experienced rejecting parents in the two workers' current moods. More often, however, we may only reach some of the warnings of violence, so that Peter can 'get off a bus and walk a long way'. Nevertheless, do not undervalue this sort of realization which can be reached gradually and will depend on some kind of relationship being established between grown-up and child. It is very rare for a child to realize the warning feelings for himself – Peter was in any case not always in time to prevent his own violence. Now and then a child may report dizziness, a momentary loss of consciousness, bright lights or strange noises which could mean an abnormal EEG, which would need investigation – it is often only from the child's communication that we can discover such phenomena.

Robert attacks *things*, but he arouses fear in adults because the *way* in which he attacks things is very terrible and personal – 'the things seem to become people'. Robert is afraid of his own violence, and the grown-ups' fear merges with his own, making him more panicky and more violent. What can one do when frightened of a violent adolescent? I think one should not try to tackle the situation alone if this can possibly be avoided – never be too proud to ask for help. If one is alone, then say and do as little as possible; be *quiet* – with luck, one may then not come into the emotional area of his violence. Never use so-called 'confrontation'. You cannot confront someone without an ego; you will only precipitate the violence, thereby losing contact with the child.

I have said very little concerning the latent nature of violence. I have been thinking about its manifest nature, and how anticipation, insight, holding and communication (both throughout the violence and after it) can all be used to manage overt violence.

My own view – based on what I have experienced and read – is that violence is primary aggression which has not been processed: that is to say, not contained, symbolized or ultimately sublimated. Obviously there is some of this primary aggression present in all of us, but not in large masses, as is the plight of many unintegrated persons.

Babies who have not had enough primary experience from their mothers experience *helpless rage*. I believe that panic violence – which sweeps the person involved off his feet – is just this *helpless rage* and the acting out of this *omnipotent violence*. A person in a state of violence is therefore both omnipotent and helpless, but the omnipotence is a denial of the helplessness. It follows that if, through verbal and non-verbal communication we can reach the helpless baby, we can establish a wavelength which may reach the original source of violence.

Chapter 18

A note on intent to murder in adolescent deprived boys

Winnicott, in a recently published posthumous collection of papers (1986), wrote, 'The theme of adolescence is death'. I have formed the same opinion as the result of many years' work in the Cotswold Community.

Among the many referred to us there is a small number of murderous boys who are more than violent, attacking adults with murderous intent. Winnicott wrote further: 'If in the fantasy of early growth there is contained death, then at adolescence there is contained murder.'

These feelings are normally contained at an unconscious level but, when children are deprived and deeply disturbed, such ideas may break through into the conscious mind, and even be acted out. These children 'with murderous intent' are not typical violent children; they are rare and dangerous.

Bettelheim has spoken of a group of homicidal youngsters encountered in the course of work at his famous Orthogenic School. He went on to say that there were children in the school who had to leave because there was no treatment for them. We have had the same experience in the Cotswold Community, where there have been attempted strangulations and attacks with such things as garden forks, causing injury to adults. The cause for the

Paper read to the therapeutic resource group in the Cotswold Community, 1987.

murderous attempts could seem to be oedipal, and the histories of such boys would suggest that this is the case. However, the murderous intent would seem to be so deeply rooted as to be unreachable by us.

In normal youngsters such feelings remain deeply in the unconscious, but in the group of which I am writing, unconscious feelings become conscious and are acted out. There is, normally, a strong barrier between conscious and unconscious, but this is not so in the group which I am trying to describe.

So far, we have found no means of understanding the nature of these boys, at referral or later. They are delinquent and emotionally deprived, but there is nothing to suggest that they are different from the other boys referred to us.

In the same way we have not found any form of special treatment for them. As and when an attack occurs which suggests murderous intent, we insulate the boy in the hope that this is an isolated incident. However, this is not normally borne out by subsequent events, although we explain to the boy concerned that if there are other dangerous attacks on adults, he will have to leave the Community.

Winnicott wrote: 'In the total unconscious fantasy belonging to growth at puberty and adolescence, there is the death of someone.' I believe that this is terribly true and that if the unconscious fantasy breaks through the barrier there will be such acting out, with murderous intent.

I have had some personal experience of this kind of problem. A boy, years ago, threw a large lump of coal at my head, which missed me by a couple of inches. The boy burst into tears and said, while still sobbing, 'I knew I had to kill you, but I'm glad that I was not able to.'

At the Cotswold Community we try to help deprived and deeply disturbed young people by the provision of primary experience, often involving regression. We have had remarkable success with many of them, but this small and dangerous group remains beyond our reach. I hope that this will not continue to be the case.

Postscript by Graham Anderson

Mrs Drysdale read the above paper to the therapeutic resource group within the Cotswold Community. There was some discussion afterwards as to the difference between an 'ordinary' panic involving violence which we would expect from an unintegrated boy and an attack with murderous intent.

From my experience, the difference is quite apparent and definite.

One day I came back from taking the Springfield boys over to the education area to find one boy still sitting at the breakfast table, the house radio playing loudly. When I turned the radio off and told the boy it was time for him to go to Poly [the Community School] he quite calmly stood up and walked to the porch. I followed down the corridor at which point he came back into the house and ran at me with a garden fork. I knew instantly that this was an extremely dangerous situation and my immediate priority was one of self-preservation. I slammed the dining-room door as the boy drove the garden fork at me. There was no doubt in my mind that but for the door I would have been seriously injured and that this was an attack with murderous intent.

When an emotionally damaged and deprived boy panics and attacks a grown-up, the aggression and anger may be diverted into symbolic communication or the boy may be reached by holding his hand and talking; if the panic is severe, he will need to be physically held and contained until the dreadful experience is completed. When a boy makes a murderous attack the situation is quite different. The attack is focused on one grown-up, the intent is clear and it is the responsibility of the grown-up involved to safeguard his own well-being. I would stress that the murderous attack is rare. This has happened only once to me during three years working in the Community. Nevertheless, the intrinsic danger of such an attack should not be underestimated, and the intent is frighteningly clear.

Postscript by Barbara Dockar-Drysdale

It will be noticed that I have written on the management of violence and on intent to murder separately. There is, for me, a gap between violence and murder, perhaps because I know a little about the management of violence, but do not believe that — at this stage of our knowledge — murderous impulses can be managed.

Chapter 19

Collusive anxiety in the residential treatment of disturbed adolescents

Collusive anxiety is a phenomenon which turns up too often in the residential treatment of delinquent adolescents. Workers are so afraid of the potential violence in their clients that they implicitly collude with their delinquent acts. This is usually achieved by 'not knowing'. There is, sometimes, what I have called a *delinquent contract*, whereby there is an unspoken understanding that, providing the grown-up does not interfere with the boy's delinquent activities, he – the boy – will be 'nice', i.e. polite and reasonable. I have seen many such 'contracts'; once trapped by this arrangement, it becomes increasingly difficult for the adult to break away without ensuring panic and disruption. Collusive anxiety is not seen only in regard to adults and boys, but also between members of a treatment team. For example, a basically violent worker may be able to keep order in a group of boys and this fact may prove of urgent importance to other adults. There need be very little actual violence; the boys must simply be aware that violence is available. The other grown-ups are too thankful for the control and apparent calm to intervene or indeed to be fully conscious of the presence of violence in a colleague who appears to be successful in his management of delinquents.

I suppose that one could draw attention to the same manifestation among parents and children. Frequently mothers collude with sons (more than with daughters) because of anxiety in regard to the father's reaction to the son's behaviour. This too is collusive anxiety, and one could say that there should *never be collusion* in family life. This can be seen in residential work, where the child care worker becomes deeply involved with the severely deprived delinquent. Here the worker rationalizes the behaviour of the delinquent and is persuaded that his behaviour is normal – in the circumstances. The more confusion in such a situation, the less likelihood there is that the delinquent will reach realization and recovery. This situation is especially difficult to encompass, because it is a fact that the adult needs to be deeply involved with the boy in order to affect him in any way. The fact is that he *must* be involved, but never at the expense of his boundaries, which need to be firmly maintained. The delinquent must be able to feel that the adult is deeply concerned, but *never* collusive.

The boys who are referred to the Cotswold Community are unintegrated. This is to say that they have not achieved a self, which is normally established by the end of the first year of life. They are, in the deepest sense of the word, deprived, lacking the provision of primary experience usually given in the course of the first year by the mother. The task of the Cotswold Community is to try to provide symbolic forms of primary experience so that the delinquent boy can at last establish himself as an individual. A boy of this kind lacks boundaries, and is therefore very liable to merge with other delinquents; he is, because of this tendency to merge, especially likely to reach states of collusive anxiety with boys in his group. For example, he will collude with a bully because he is afraid of being bullied himself.

Unintegrated boys suffer from attacks of *panic*; often anxiety can grow into panic at which point it becomes *unthinkable anxiety*. Such panic states can lead to violent acting out, sometimes by a single boy, but often by a merger of several in collusion with a leader of whom they are afraid. I once experienced a very strange example of this in the Mulberry Bush School. Four boys of about ten years old made a cardboard fort in their lesson group. The fort became populated by little rubber monsters (who could be stuck on the end of pencils). The leader of the four boys – Anthony – owned an especially horrible little monster called Gruesome. All four boys were terrified of Gruesome, whom Anthony took to bed with him, hiding him under his pillow.

Gradually, all the boys became very frightened of the monsters. They all projected their own violence on to the monsters, where the violence merged and returned *against* the boys. However, they clung together and used the monsters to threaten other children. The climate became so emotionally loaded that we had to intervene. After much discussion and thought we introduced a Society for the Protection of Unhappy Monsters. There was also a hospital for them. The boys became involved in these activities and gradually emerged from their collusive anxiety through caring for the monsters.

Recently, the Ombudsman of Alberta (Canada) was asked to investigate complaints about a well-known establishment for residential treatment of disturbed youngsters. This is in fact an excellent place – I've visited there myself – but there was one factor of which I was unaware. The establishment had a quiet room in which children were isolated for considerable lengths of time. The Ombudsman produced a very fine report, which did not condemn the institution, but did make clear that there could be no more use of this quiet room technique. Now the point I wish to make is that people were going in and out of this place either as workers or as visitors and yet, until this crisis, nobody had expressed any anxiety. The institution was well established; presumably no one dared to bring accusations against treatment methods, although many people must have known that 'quiet rooms' were not therapeutic. In fact, collusive anxiety must exist all over the place. We may well be sure that, in such circumstances, we would speak out and demand reform. I am not too certain that this is true. In fact, the people who do criticize a place tend to be very paranoid workers, whose accusations are quite unjustified. It is difficult to assess the origins of collusive anxiety. I find myself thinking of Anna Freud's 'identification with the object of fear'. Certainly this would explain some aspects of collusive anxiety.

I have already referred to the situation where a mother identifies in a collusive way with a son against a father. I think there are many such instances; perhaps this is one of the special problems linked with the treatment of delinquents. Workers actually collude with delinquent clients where they have been seduced by the client's charm: at the same time the worker is *afraid* of the client.

I remember, a few years ago, being asked by an Inspector for ideas as to how a room should be furnished in which an adolescent would be confined. I answered that I could make no suggestions, as I found it quite intolerable to imagine a young person being locked up alone. I said that I thought the furnishing of such a room was unimportant, providing that a known and trusted adult could be locked up with the child. I think, in fact, that this is the only way in which collusive anxiety can be challenged. We call this 'open communication' at the Cotswold Community. This means that there is an insignificant amount of subculture, because everything, however painful, is surfaced and discussed.

I realize that there may be many practices in our own culture which we may find abhorrent, but collusive anxiety – in this case fear of losing one's job – can ensure silence. However, there can be circumstances in which collusion can be justified. For example, a priest who worked with delinquents in Naples some time ago never criticized his clients, however delinquent they might be, until he had really come to know them. The primary task for him was to establish communication. In such a case there is collusion for special reasons, but not out of anxiety or a need for quiet.

Another situation in which collusive anxiety is not easy to avoid would be one in which one's life is actually at risk. For example, if one's country were occupied by a foreign power it would not be wrong to learn to talk to the enemy at one's door.

This is very much the problem in residential treatment where one delinquent boy can become a 'hero' and a 'storm centre' (Redl, 1966). Other children are so afraid of this boy that they dare not reveal what has been happening, even when they have been badly hurt and frightened.

So I would be quite sure that direct and open communication is essential in every residential place, so that at no time will children or their caring people be dominated by collusive anxiety.

Chapter 20

Staff consultation in an evolving care system

This paper is an attempt to describe an on-going project. Our task was to set up a therapeutic structure within an existing management structure. We hope that the structure will be strong enough to support staff through considerable change, to reach a new position.

The workers concerned are the usual mixture of different personalities and skills, and are trained or untrained. It seems to me that this sort of therapeutic structure could be set up in most caring institutions.

I have recently reached a tentative realization which seems to throw considerable light on problems which I have only partially understood in the course of my work as a consultant. I think of this realization of mine as 'the theory of the impossible task', the 'theory' being the basic assumption that people cannot change except in superficial ways, an idea subscribed to by families, institutions and managing bodies (see Chapter 6). Child care workers are praised and admired as unselfish, dedicated people making great sacrifices in order to devote themselves to a hopeless but worthy cause. This encouraging, praising attitude continues through all sorts of crises, breakdowns and failures, but changes to anxiety and suspicion should any success attend the struggles of the people involved in this kind of work.

The theory of the impossible task is to be found among child care workers themselves. Some people actually choose this kind of work just because they believe it to be impossible – like climbers assailing a peak which they believe to be unconquerable.

Long ago, I remember, there was a student at the Mulberry Bush who could not manage a play group of three disturbed children. She left us after a few weeks, and, when we next had news of her, she was working for an organization aimed at achieving world peace. I also remember, to give another instance, the young wife of a new member of staff at the Cotswold Community telling me, 'But this way of working is not possible.'

This basic assumption was one of the many obstacles which I encountered when I started to work as a consultant in the Cotswold Community not that I recognized the nature of the obstacle at that time. I only knew that I was being made to feel 'helpless and hopeless' and that there was more than one barrier between myself and the workers in the place; realization came later.

Another obstacle lay in the survival of what I ultimately termed 'the Dinosaurs' – a subculture of institutionalization based on the past hierarchical structure which was giving place to a therapeutic community. There were many adults and boys who believed that the change was momentary and that the old order would be restored before long. The Dinosaur was made up of all the bits of institutionalization remaining in the people living in the place. For example, the attitude to night care remained entrenched in the past (when there was a night-watchman), change being fiercely resisted for a long time. One could say that there was a deep relief in a return to the 'institutional womb'.

The third realization which helped me to understand the problems a bit better was what I called 'the fallacy of a delusional equilibrium'. This was another basic assumption on the part of many people in the place, which implied that by keeping things calm and smooth on top, the chaos below the surface need not be reached. Breakdown in this false equilibrium was projected on to any likely scapegoat.

When I started work, the first fundamental changes had been brought about already. I am going to quote a brief unpublished report which I wrote concerning my work during this early period in the Cotswold Community.

Initially we saw my tasks to be (firstly) the provision of ego support in order to facilitate ego functioning in integrated children; (secondly) the containment of unintegrated children with provision of primary experience with which to build the self and achieve integration. These two tasks were to be carried out through work with both staff and boys. It was assumed that unintegrated children would form a small minority group in the place; this group would need, as soon as possible, to be insulated in order to receive appropriate treatment. The mixture of integrated and unintegrated boys was recognized as undesirable.

In the event, I was assigned to a house, St David's, consisting of very deprived and disturbed boys; this group was not yet separated in any way from the rest of the Community, but was self-selective in terms of gross disturbance as a common factor. I talked with the boys and with the staff individually, until the staff themselves asked for group meetings with me. These staff groups became the nucleus of my work in the Community. My sessions with boys could – with their permission – be used to help staff to gain insight and to understand the need for team-work in order to provide experience. These individual sessions were – and remain – of necessity brief (twenty to thirty minutes). I have found that, where residential workers are themselves carrying out a therapeutic programme, sessions with individual boys have what I call a 'key' function, helping to open and deepen channels of communication between boys and workers.

St David's became presently the unit for unintegrated boys known as 'the Cottage'. Once this kind of insulation had been established, my task became more precise. By discussing weekly 'happenings' chosen by the Cottage team, I was able to help them to provide primary experience through individual adaptation to need, based on early dependence and involving localized regression within a relationship in a firmly structured containing environment. In this way, the team came to realize how disciplined any real therapeutic work must be and to be aware of the danger of collusion and the need for confrontation of a non-punitive kind. The team did good work, although naturally making many mistakes which with adequate support they could face. The development of an ego culture in the Cottage minimized authoritarian attitudes at one extreme and subcultures at the other. The establishment of open communication between staff and boys reduced acting out; and the insulation and containment of this group of unintegrated boys enabled ego growth and strengthening in other groups within the Community.

For various reasons it was decided after a time that I should work in a similar consultant-tutor role in the remaining three house teams. My weekly discussion groups evolved into seminars, with learning based on the group experiences during the current week. Each group seminar lasts for forty-five minutes, with periods of from twenty to thirty minutes available as before for key sessions with boys, usually at their own request, and for tutorials with team members – often the heads of houses. I have a close liaison with the head of group living, who plans my day's work each week, and with whom I discuss my work in detail each Wednesday evening on the telephone, after my return home. I have also meetings with Mike Jinks, the head of education. I meet Richard Balbernie (the head of the Community) frequently and discuss problems and recommendations with him, both there and by telephone.

The development of a system of need assessment has enabled us to chart all houses on a basis of integrated or unintegrated; and, if unintegrated, to chart the specific syndrome of deprivation. From this 'inside diagnosis' we are now in a position to plan treatment on a foundation of need and to select with some certainty those boys to whom we can offer help. The work on need assessment is also enabling the staff to conceptualize and communicate what they are doing; and recently teams have begun to carry out these assessments themselves, checking results with me, so that we can plan treatment programmes in an exact way.

In order to understand the nature of the task facing a consultant in this particular set of circumstances, it seems important to clarify the nature of a classification such as I have just mentioned, that is, into integrated and unintegrated. To quote from my own work:

Winnicott and others have postulated a primary state of unity of the mother and her baby. In thinking about emotional deprivation I find it necessary to take as a starting point this state of unity at the beginning of a baby's life. Freud wrote, 'For, just as the mother originally satisfied all the needs of the foetus through the apparatus of her own body, so now, after its birth, she continues to do so, though partly through other means. There is much more continuity between intra-uterine life and earliest infancy than the impressive caesura of the act of birth would have us believe' (1926, p. 138). In the course of normal development the separating out of mother and baby is a long and gradual process; at the completion of this the baby exists for the first time as a separate individual, absolutely dependent on the mother, but no longer emotionally part of her. If integration of the personality is to take place, usually by the end of the first year of life, the evolution of this process must not be interrupted. Interruption of this essential process, which mothers and babies work through together in their own time and in their own way, is in my view the trauma which lies at the root of the various types of cases of emotional deprivation referred to us.

The point at which traumatic interruption has taken place determines the nature of the survival mechanisms used by the child; the primitive nature of these mechanisms does not prevent them from being used in a highly complex manner. Winnicott has said: 'All the rest of mental illness (other than psycho-neurosis) belongs to the build-up of the personality in earliest childhood and in infancy, along with the environmental provision that fails or succeeds in its function of facilitating the maturational processes of the individual. In other words, mental illness that is not psycho-neurosis has importance for the social worker because it concerns not so much the individual's organized defences as the individual's failure to attain the ego-strength or the personality integration that enables defences to form' (1965, pp. 219–20). The emotionally deprived child is pre-neurotic, unable to experience guilt or anxiety, and functioning at various primitive stages of development. For a neurotic child there may have been inadequate continuity between the intra-uterine and postnatal phases, but nevertheless he has enough protective and protected environment to make it possible for him to build a separate personality structure, capable of integrating good and bad experiences and his responses to them, rather than being helplessly buffeted by them. He is thus able, having reached integration because of 'good enough infant care' (Winnicott, 1958, p. 212) to embark on the long voyage of secondary experience. (Dockar-Drysdale, 1968, p. 98)

When we first classified all the boys in the Cotswold Community on the basis of integration as individuals, we found that 75 per cent of our population turned out to be unintegrated. This was a rough-and-ready emergency classification, using the presence of panic and disruption as the factors determining whether or not a boy was to be considered integrated. A unit for the integrated 25 per cent was set up, which accepted boys who achieved integration as the result of treatment within the Community and those, a very few, who on referral seemed to be integrated. Obviously, my work with the staff of the unit for integrated boys (Boulderstone) was very different from discussions with teams in other units.

Initially, as I have indicated, subject matter for team discussion groups depended entirely on what they themselves surfaced. I felt that they were under such stress that my chief value at first must be as a safety valve in what was a crisis culture. There was mass acting out in all units, and subculture among staff as well as boys. Workers, both in groups and individually, selected communication to impart to me in a way which made it very difficult to be of any use. The fallacy of the delusional equilibrium, already mentioned, was much in evidence: information concerning the various units gave the impression of a smooth-running, well-established organization, disturbed only by the not-to-be-explained phenomena of acting out, which could not be denied.

So I did what I could with the limited resources at my disposal, often bored and frustrated, but hoping that as workers came to know and trust me, more urgent reality could begin to be communicated.

In fact, the process of classifying as 'integrated' or 'unintegrated' did much to open up dialogue. In order to answer the questions 'Does this boy panic?' and 'Does he disrupt?', workers started to ask themselves new questions about boys and about themselves. In order to make use of this development I evolved a technique which

I call 'Need Assessment'. The use of this kind of technique seems to me to be essential in focusing, as it does, the attention of the whole group including the consultant on the primary task – in our case, the provision of primary experience.

On the basis that anti-task, acting out and subcultures of all kinds tend to spring from a breakdown in real communication, it would seem of the utmost importance to keep all lines of communication open – between members of the team, between grown-ups and children and between the consultant and all others in the place. The making of a Need Assessment involves the whole staff group of a residential unit, working with the consultant and pooling resources in order to evaluate need. Often insights are reached in the making of these assessments which are of value not only to the child under consideration, but also to the treatment team themselves, throwing light on problems of delusional countertransference – splitting mechanisms, for example – but in a way which is tolerable because it is indirect and shared.

Such an approach seems to me to give child care workers a proper professional position in the scheme of things, the consultant being entirely dependent on the material brought forward by the unit team (see Chapter 22).

The questions asked in the Need Assessment are those which I have asked myself in attempting to analyse a Context Profile, which is a method of reporting by the team on experience with one child during a week.

I have tried to approach the problem of meeting the child's needs – whatever these may be – by classification (rather than by considering his symptoms). I think that it would always be necessary for a senior worker to lead such a group discussion, asking and explaining the questions and recording the answers. There can be no 'yes' or 'no' answers; all replies must be based on actual experiences with the child.

We have found that this kind of Need Assessment helps us in planning for the child's management and care. A Need Assessment in no way replaces other assessments (case history, intellectual ability and so on). I find it a valuable addition to other information.

The questions can be answered for the first time only by a group of people who are living with the child and have been doing so for at least three weeks or a month: they must understand that this is a *first* Need Assessment – that there will be others necessary in order to meet the child's evolving needs. I think that only a group of resident workers can draw on the kind of experience essential to this type of assessment.

One individual can make this sort of assessment. An Assessment when completed forms a basis for a treatment programme. The other less obvious use of Need Assessments is the introduction of important concepts to staff, always in a practical context, so that workers quite easily become accustomed to considering boys in this rather exact and disciplined way and to applying the concepts to themselves as well as to the boys.

The Assessments are of course repeated at intervals and are always available for reference. The material required is from personal experience, so that pseudo–objectivity in the form of observation 'out there' is avoided.

As the unit teams became accustomed to using Need Assessments, there was a considerable opening up of communication, especially because, for the first time, people began to take some share of responsibility for boys' acting out. I felt it was safe to say – and say again – that all acting out results from breakdown in communication. The exception to this statement can be found in symbolic acting out in relation to an adult. This is acting out *towards* communication, and can turn up in the course of treatment. The distinction is clear because this special acting out is always directed to a known and trusted person, whereas acting out which is broken–down communication is quite anonymous and concerns unknown people.

The realization of this fact produced an almost intolerable level of anxiety among the workers; but honesty, courage and determination led them to investigate the boys' acting out so that in most cases we could actually find the point at which communication broke down. This particular realization came with others, in such a way that workers began to accept professional and personal responsibility for crisis situations. They began to consider ways in which acting out and violence could be anticipated and often prevented or at least be localized.

People working with unintegrated children and adolescents have to carry a much heavier load of tension and anxiety than those who are trying to help neurotic, integrated youngsters. Workers at the Cotswold Community are constantly exposed to the full blast of primary processes: they are in touch with what should be in the unconscious but which, without ego development, is present at a conscious level in all its primitive violence (Winnicott used to describe this as 'dreaming awake'). The danger – apart from the actual violent acting out – is that this primitive material can pick up wavelengths in the unconscious of the workers. This is what can lead to collusive pairing, which is damaging in the extreme to boy and adult. For these reasons it is essential that workers should become as conscious as possible about themselves, so that they and the boys are less at risk and more free to concentrate on the primary task. Some time ago there was an outburst of acting out by certain boys and, in the course of sorting out the causes, the following fact, among many, came to light.

A student took three boys in her car to the nearest town: one boy sat in front, two behind. On the back seat of the car was the student's bag with money in it. The boys asked her to move this bag, as they found it too much of a strain to have it on the seat beside them. The student laughed and said that she was not worried, leaving the bag where it was. Later, the boys stole money from the bag and went on to further delinquency. The student did not initially tell me about the bag. When she eventually did, she reported it all without guilt. It came to her as a great and quite genuine shock to find that she had triggered off a delinquent explosion in a collusive way.

This was a very obvious example of unconscious collusion. There are many more subtle and hidden ways in which this sort of mechanism can operate, but only as long as the worker remains unconscious of it. The surfacing of such material puts an end to the unconscious technique which cannot now be employed without guilt.

Presently, staff teams began to understand just how important communication could be. This realization made it possible for me to introduce the idea of 'talking groups'. Morning meetings of total groups (staff and boys) had not proved successful prior to classification. It now seemed that, while integrated boys could communicate in this sort of setting, unintegrated boys were unable to tolerate the high degree of stress, becoming disruptive, withdrawn or panicky. The integrated boys in Boulderstone could stand this experience, while those in the other units could come together with staff for information to be imparted to them (plans, etc.) without too much strain. For the purpose of inter-communication, I suggested the introduction of very small groups (four boys to one adult). In this setting all boys became able to exchange communication, and these small groups have continued to function with a reasonable degree of success. Of course, talking groups did not replace deeply personal communication between a boy and a grown-up, sometimes spontaneous but more often planned for a definite short span of time in each day, usually at bedtime.

At this point, therefore, the staff groups with which I was working formulated Need Assessments with me for all boys, carried out the recommendations of the Assessments and ran small talking groups. They discussed all these activities with me, both individually and in groups, and gradually deepened this under-standing of delinquency equating with deprivation. In parallel, Richard Balbernie and Isabel Menzies were also making workers more conscious and responsible. The people in the place were therefore going through a very difficult period of growing awareness, both individually and in groups.

During this period I added twenty-four-hour programmes to our established Need Assessments. The whole group went over twenty-four hours with me in respect of the needs of an individual boy – for example, how he needed to be woken in the morning. A programme like this ensured that a unit team would all know a boy's needs at that time, so that newcomers could quickly gain information. Changes in the programme could be recorded. This twenty-four-hour programme has proved to be especially valuable for new boys on arrival (prior to actual need assessment).

All this is in the context of a management structure which divides sixty boys into groups of from nine to fourteen persons, in four units. Each unit has a head, a senior house-mother and two or three others, any one of whom may be called on to substitute for the head. One of these units caters for integrated boys, three for unintegrated. Usually the integrated boys have achieved integration within the Community.

The needs of each boy must be formally assessed by the team group within the first month, and thereafter at intervals of about three months. Ways of meeting these needs must be found within the management structure (in terms of working hours of staff, life-style of unit, etc.). At present we do not have adequate referral assessments. Integrated boys will not require need assessment so much as good reporting. Within this management structure, a therapeutic structure must exist. Selection of staff depends on personality, training and experience. In the one unit for integrated boys, staff will need to be ego-supportive; in the other three units they will need to be ego-providing (that is to say, you cannot support what is not there).

This classification is the initial structure required for therapy to take place, in order to carry out the two primary tasks in the place: provision for integrated and provision for unintegrated boys. Such classification can fit comfortably within the management structure.

Within the therapeutic main structure are the substructures. Therapy can take place within many fields: food, bedtime and getting up, school, communication, play, bathing, clothes and others. In each and every case, however, the therapeutic structure must contain the therapy, which must also fit into the management structure: if, for example, 'lights out' is at ten o'clock, this is not the moment to start therapeutic communication with boys. Equally, no therapeutic structure could exist within a management structure which sends most staff off at weekends. The use of 'weekends' is an obvious example of the need for a management structure within which a therapeutic structure *can* fit. Night care is another example.

In the unit for integrated boys we can think in terms of a group. Here the whole group could meet daily with the team to discuss the problems in the unit and reach decisions. We can assume an ego nucleus or ego functioning (they will also need other forms of communication).

In no other units is there a group (the false group structure in one unit led to breakdown in communication and to subculture). These unintegrated units need what Winnicott called 'cover'. We find, however, that small talking groups (four boys to one adult) with separate lifelines to the adult *do* lead to communication.

The small talking groups can be contained within the management structure and form part of the therapeutic structure; within the talking groups, matters to do with inner reality can surface safely.

These groups have no part to play in management, that is, decisions are not reached – the aim is not to make decisions but to facilitate open communications. There can be house groups of staff and boys for all sorts of communication, and this is not therapy but good management. The large meeting in Boulderstone also fits within the management structure, but has an objective social purpose and can reach decisions. In all units there is opportunity for one-to-one communication, often at bedtime. This must be structured to fit within management.

All therapeutic communication needs to take place between the same people, at the same time, in the same place and for the same duration. This time and place structure must fit into management. Of course there is unplanned, casual communication in context, at any time. Within the 'Polytechnic' area there is plenty of planned communication, both individual and in small groups.

Every boy should have opportunities for individual and group communication daily. This is the only answer to unintegrated subculture and acting out. Every bit of acting out can be traced to a breakdown in communication. Unintegrated boys need a structure to contain: (1) regular small talking groups; (2) individual communication with an adult; and (3) immediate communication in context.

Twenty-four-hour management programmes are needed for all unintegrated boys, to ensure reliable continuity of provision in a unit. Here again, twenty-four-hour programmes must fit into the main management structure of the whole place and of the unit, otherwise programmes will break down. Equally, any change of management must respect programmes.

Localization of provision is essential, and indeed without localization therapeutic work of this kind is impossible. Ten minutes, properly used, are more valuable than two hours of permissive 'floating'. Primary provision must be individual – one cannot provide localized regression or adaptation for a group, but only for individuals in a group with adequate cover for all.

Play. Many unintegrated boys cannot play in a way appropriate to their age. They will, however, play in a sand heap, with small toys on a play tray, in dens or tents and with soft toys in bed. A play tray should have a small box of toys for the particular boy. A soft toy should be made for him, if requested, and should be cared for and mended. Therapeutic play should also take place in a regular, structured way – not just anywhere, at any time, with anyone.

Food. This of course is an invaluable field for primary provision, but it must never be depersonalized. Eggs at breakfast can be cooked to individual requirements without causing difficulties of management. Midday meals in a canteen are not therapeutic, but are appropriate for integrated boys as a social experience. If midday meals must be centralized, then at least efforts should be made to give complete experiences (for example, a whole small jelly). Food adaptations must sometimes be specially arranged with management (for example, a sack of apples for Keith).

The Poly (the school). Here there is a particular problem in that boys are not classified as integrated or unintegrated in terms of group arrangement. Essentially, the Poly must be concerned with ego-functioning elements. Where these are not – or are barely – present, it is a question whether a boy should be in any group learning situation. It would seem that, for the more unintegrated boys, 'lifelines' must be arranged (for example, individual remedial settings). One could imagine two parts of the Poly, if this were practical. Obviously, the integrated people in Boulderstone should function well in group situations of learning and living.

All therapy requires a close and deep relationship between boy and worker. Adaptation 'dosage' would do harm. There can be no depersonalized care, whatever the boy may feel about the worker. The worker must remain concerned about the boy, even when hated by him. Vague dishing out of 'tea and sympathy' is not therapeutic work. All provision must have symbolic realization. Any therapeutic structure assumes that this is already understood. There are many therapeutic techniques not available in the circumstances: we must make good use of what we *can* do. For example, verbal interpretation often cannot be used with our very ill clients. It will then be what we do rather than what we say that can be of use to them: but what we do must be planned, realistic and reliable.

One of the factors which tend to make workers feel helpless is their conviction that it would be inappropriate for them to make interpretations to the boys in their care. This conclusion often immobilizes them and prevents further efforts towards other goals. While I would agree that deep interpretation should not be used by unanalysed people, however, talented, symbolic communication remains at their disposal and is often of considerable use in their therapeutic work.

To give a simple example: a boy draws a small house surrounded by a high wall. The therapist may well comment: 'The person who owns that house must feel safe inside those high walls – but can he see the countryside beyond them?' Such a comment may lead to a dialogue which will have a lot to do with the crippling nature of the boy's defences, but which can remain in the context of the picture. There are now many workers in the Cotswold who can use this sort of technique extremely well. They also acquire the art of therapeutic listening – listening to a boy's communication with the whole of themselves, to the exclusion of all else – which is not easy.

One of the most difficult tasks which I have undertaken in working as a consultant to a 'caring establishment' is what I think of as coping with 'the Crunch'. The crunch means for me the collision of objective with inner reality, and can perhaps best be explained by example. Jim, a boy at the Cotswold became interested in chess, so that presently he wished to carve a chess set. He made a king, a queen and a pawn, which he brought to show me. His instructor told me that he now refused to complete the set. However, Jim *had*, from his point of view, completed another kind of set: a father, a mother and a child – the family life he had never known. It is difficult for workers to accept this other kind of reality, especially when there is such a clash of interests and investment.

Recently, a boy who had great problems of communication started to play squiggles with me. He turned all my squiggles into strange creatures which lived underwater. (One of these creatures was large, round, soft and pink: it had lost its mouth at the bottom of the river. This was his mother's breast, and the lost mouth was his own, which had lost her breast. Now he attributed the mouth *to her breast*.) I spoke a little about this material to a colleague, saying that it would be terrible if somebody was to teach him about real underwater life at this point. A few days later Peter turned a squiggle into something amorphous. He said with marked hesitation, 'Something like jelly with black dots . . .' and went on to try to speak about tadpoles, in a muddled and hesitant voice, such as he usually employs – quite different from the easy flow of his underwater voice. I asked, 'Has someone been explaining to you about tadpoles and all that?' He said that his teacher had taken him to the pond and had shown him frog spawn and so forth. I observed that I thought *his* creatures lived in much deeper water: he was able to make use of this comment and the next squiggle took him back to the creatures of his inner reality.

There was another child, long ago, who used to ask me, 'What does one and one make?' The answer was 'one' (the child as part of his mother). This incorrect arithmetic was very important to him just at that time.

I think 'the Crunch' between objective and inner reality explains some of the problems faced by teachers and therapists working together. At the Cotswold Community we are trying to see the importance of both realities, so that one is not sacrificing one for the other at certain moments of conflict. In dealing with unintegrated children, internal reality must be established before objective reality can be recognized.

There have been further developments. There is now in each unit a manager, a management continuity resource person, a therapeutic resource person, one or two educational skill resource people and one or two team members. The therapeutic resource person is responsible for twenty-four-hour programmes, Context Profiles (a detailed type of reporting on a boy for a week by the whole team), Need Assessments, talking groups and communication plans, adaptations to individual needs and therapeutic play. Richard Balbernie and I meet the therapeutic resource people (there are four, one to each unit) weekly to discuss their work. There is also a training group which I run each week for newcomers to the place; and a group run by Richard Balbernie and myself for staff wives (this last has proved to be essential).

I feel we have achieved a therapeutic structure which has evolved in a gradual and realistic way. There are in all this great hazards and problems which sometimes seem insuperable. I have spoken of some of the difficulties – of the presence of the shadowy Dinosaur surviving from the institutional past; the presence from time to time of anti-task, often represented by some new members of a group; selective communication so that some things are not allowed to surface in discussion with me (I could not work without communication from Richard Balbernie); and delusional equilibrium – the thin ice which is so smooth and deceptive with chaos beneath.

There are other problems, difficult to recognize, let alone solve. For example, it can be very hard to diagnose a delinquent pairing of an adult with a boy which can look like a conscious therapeutic involvement. It is very difficult to assess just how much insight workers can tolerate without becoming immobilized by anxiety. It is not at the moment that insight is gained, but later, when the worker discovers changes in himself, that a danger point can be reached – when, for example, long-established crisis avoidance techniques can no longer be unconsciously employed. There is an almost opposite risk, however, when a worker accepts and 'learns' a theoretical concept without 'digestion'; he introjects but does not incorporate the idea within himself in terms of his own experience. A worker who does this word-swallowing trick will produce the concept just as it went into him, present it to others – his colleagues and the boys who are his clients – in such a way that it will be rightly and bitterly resisted because they will not feel 'real'.

I have also found myself making a blunder which I call 'opening the oven door while the cake is rising'. By this I mean that it is disastrous to conceptualize some part of a process through which the worker may be living at that time. Experience must be realized and symbolized before it can be conceptualized. Premature conceptualization by a consultant can interrupt and possibly stop a process which is dynamic and necessary for the worker's evolvement.

If I accept an introjecting person as an incorporating one I run the risk of supporting a worker who *says* all the right things while continuing to go his own way, doing what he has always done.

This kind of person stays up half the night talking with a boy, without resentment and without guilt, because it never occurs to him that he is getting pleasure from this himself. The introduction of structure into his work – the realization that a complete experience lasting twenty minutes (with a beginning, a middle and an end) can be therapeutic in a way in which hours of talk may never be – interrupts a well-established drift towards collusive pairing, producing fierce resistance. In these circumstances the worker accepts the theory (by word-swallowing) but continues the long, drifting talks even though he may now feel that this is delinquent (because this has been demonstrated to him). He continues, but he feels guilt. I think this is important to understand: insight will arouse personal guilt in areas where there has been none before. Obviously, the worker will be very anxious and resentful, so that I sometimes meet a lot of anger at this point. Equally, the worker may take flight (Richard Balbernie calls this the 'good tomorrow syndrome'). I find that I must be very careful not to surface too much at any time, never more than can be tolerated and incorporated in a gradual way.

Of course, there are the more familiar phenomena: envy of me as the consultant, sometimes dealt with by identification with me as a psychotherapist; and devaluation of the consultant in which I am played along in a patronizing way with everyone being 'nice to me'. There are also accusations against the institution, some of which are really unconsciously directed against me.

I am not doing group therapy, so I leave transference alone and do not make interpretations. Occasionally a worker really needs professional help while going through some specially difficult experience – he may be very distressed and confused. In this event, I may refer him at his own request to a colleague, usually in London, for a period of psychotherapy. This works well and prevents people using colleagues as therapists. I do myself meet workers alone, usually at their request, to sort out less acute difficulties.

Recently we have added to the therapeutic structuring. It seemed absolutely necessary to assess the amount of ego strength present in any unit, in order to judge what sort of boys could be safely admitted. With the help of others in the Community, we now have a kind of chart which evaluates ego strength in each boy and in the whole group within a unit. Should this strength fall below a specific level, we can know that the unit is at risk.

Syndromes of deprivation are graded in terms of ego strength: for example, a frozen boy scores 1, while a caretaker syndrome scores 4. Since we are now in a position from which we can assess the syndromes within any unit, we can also score – roughly – the ego strength. On occasions when the ego strength drops below the minimum level required, the team ego-nucleus has to be drawn on if the unit is to survive. This leads to impoverishment of grown-ups and eventually to breakdown. The team can now say, for example, 'We cannot admit a frozen boy when we next have a vacancy; our score would be too low.' We are even learning what combination of such syndromes produces a working group (for example, there cannot be more than one new frozen boy in a group).

Richard Balbernie, the therapeutic resource people and myself have also evolved a way of scoring communication rating. A communication level of 'A' indicates that the boy is able to talk about himself with real feeling – personally – and about his problems. A level of 'B' would usually be about current affairs in the unit or in the Community. 'C' would be superficial chatter.

A week of communication at 'C' level by a boy, as rated by most people, would suggest a risk of breakdown into acting out, and would indicate the need for special steps to be taken to reach more real communication.

To summarize: *Need Assessments* provide a basis for planning treatment for the individual boy as well as classifying the particular syndrome of deprivation. *Treatment programmes* cover the twenty-four hours in the daily life of each boy, so that everyone in the unit knows the agreed approach in everyday situations to each boy. *Talking groups* are small groups, meeting with the same adult in the same place, and facilitate communication and lessen the risk of acting out. *Communication rating* makes it possible to judge the current level of communication of the individual and of the group. *Ego scoring* adds up the ego strength in any unit in order to make sure that at least the minimal required ego strength is possible. *Therapeutic resource workers* introduce and maintain a therapeutic structure within the management structure of each unit. *Educational need assessments* assess the underlying educational needs in deprived children (for example, problems of perception).

All these techniques help to make staff more aware of what they are doing, responsible and less likely to project their own inevitable failures on to the boys. People may now say 'We are feeling awful' instead of 'The boys are being terrible'. An example of acceptance of responsibility by workers is the fact that they have gradually grown accustomed to the idea that they must keep notes on any regular sessions with individual boys. These notes are made available to the consultant and to the group for discussion from time to time. When I first made this requirement it was apparently accepted, but actually bypassed by various means – often on the grounds that there was not enough time available to make notes; in another case the worker reported what the boy had said but none of his own comments.

My aim has been to allow people to experience, to reach realization and to conceptualize, rather than to bog down in panic which is lit only by gleams of intuition – a state which can force workers to depersonalize and disassociate, as in the Dinosaur subculture.

There are bound to be elements of 'crisis culture' in a community such as the Cotswold Community, so that 'in the circumstances' can often be used with some validity as an escape from responsibility. However, it seems that the more precise and definite the therapeutic structure, the less likely it is to collapse in an emergency: people get into conscious difficulties rather than a collusive muddle, so that they remain responsible for problems, rather than investing collusive muddle in boys.

I have described difficulties, but I would not be presenting reality if I did not stress the fact that the workers in the Cotswold Community reach a very high standard of therapeutic work. It used to be supposed by many people that such work could be carried out only by trained psychotherapists already analysed – nothing could be further from the case. Despite the pain of gaining insight, the acute anxiety aroused by accepting responsibility, in the deepest sense, for other people's acting out, the people in the place continue to tolerate a learning process which demands so much of them; and continue to work in a way which calls for respect and admiration. The changes and evolvement in the boys which take place as a result of their efforts can be seen clearly in later Need Assessments: this gives workers a satisfaction greater by far than anything they have experienced in the past, because it is not polluted by collusion and subculture.

These people are beginning to prove that the task is not impossible. It remains to be seen whether society can tolerate the realization that change *is* possible in anti-social adolescents – and in themselves.

Chapter 21

The problem of making adaptation to the needs of the individual child in a group

The problem of meeting the needs of individual children in a group situation is one which everybody who works closely with children must experience sooner or later. It is one of the most difficult and frustrating situations in residential work to find oneself in, having established contact with a particular child on an individual basis, unable to carry this over into life in the group. The opportunities for work with individual children are usually few and far between, so that it is only too easy for the fragile bond between grown-up and child to be broken in the stress and strain of the group situation before it is even really established. Such a state of things is, of course, extremely bad for the child concerned, and equally disastrous for the grown-up. Is it possible to manage to strengthen such a bond despite all the obvious difficulties involved?

I am not in this paper discussing the very special form of adaption belonging to one phase of a total regression, which, in any case, I call conscious involvement rather than adaption and have discussed elsewhere. I felt that it would only be confusing to consider involvement in the context of group work because the deepest phase of a total regression must take place between a

First published in *New Trends in Child Care: The Magazine of the RCCA* 9, 1961.

grown-up and a child with emotional support, and is something very different from anything which can take place in a group.

I am not discussing group therapy because that is work which I would feel to be dependent on a nucleus of ego strength in some or all members of the group, on which the therapist can depend. It would be impossible, for example, to do real group therapy with psychotic children, although a therapist could be working with several psychotic children who happened to be in one room at the same time. In the same way, children who have had little or no opportunity for satisfactory emotional experience may seem to be together in a group, but are really utterly isolated from each other, with no inner resources to pool with those of the therapist. It is adaption to the needs of this kind of child that I am considering.

The mother with a new-born baby is in a state of unity; she is for the time being, also, in a state of near perfect adaption to her baby, she does not have to *make* an adaptation deliberately; there is no conflict, no problem involved, because what the baby needs is what she needs.

A grown-up living in a residential setting with a group of children cannot, and in fact should not, become adapted in this sort of way, although this might be precisely what is being demanded of the grown-up by the child. I think this is often a very hard fact to face, because the grown-up may well feel a great need to cede to a child's demands, to become involved in a situation comparable to that of a mother with her new-born baby, because this state of adaption is a deeply satisfying state of things – at all events at first – for grown-up and child; especially because the grown-up is able to feel that he, or she, is giving the child all it needs, and the child is feeling that at last here is everything, the whole world, the universe – his for the taking – and more and more and more.

Now, I have watched this sort of process take place in residential treatment, and such stories do not have a happy ending for anybody concerned. Very soon there is intense resentment felt by other members of the staff who are not themselves in a state of adaption and do not wish to be, and who feel – in fact, quite rightly – that there is something which is not quite right about such a situation, which tends to be extremely disruptive both to other grown-ups and other children.

Presently, also, the adapted grown-up reaches the limits of endurance and suddenly feels that he or she is losing identity and becoming lost in the child, whose demands become more and more omnipotent. At the same time the child becomes panicky, because as one child said to me recently, 'Everything is really the same as nothing, and if I get absolutely everything there would be nothing at all.'

At this stage several things can happen. The grown-up may suddenly withdraw from the situation, having become suddenly aware of a need for self-preservation; may modify his or her attitude and refuse to meet demands; in order to keep the whole thing going, the grown-up and the child may isolate themselves in a little world of their own, regarding everybody else as enemies; or the grown-up may have some sort of physical collapse. One thing is sure, and that is that infinite adaption to the demands of such a child is an impossibility, and the various breakdowns which I have described lead to chaos for everybody in the environment, because when something of this sort happens, the child, in a frenzied panic, destroys everything within reach. I know that I have painted a gloomy picture here, but I feel that there is a very real danger that people working with children can undervalue what they are doing because they feel that to be therapeutic is to be permissive and that they are at the time falling short of what is needed, whereas, in fact, they are probably doing extremely well and giving a great deal of help to children.

I think we must all face the fact – whatever our particular work may be – that we are not going to be able to give a child everything he needs all the time. It would also be true to say that this applies to mothers with their babies, and that failure to meet needs becomes an important factor in emotional growth and, while failure in adaptation is inevitable, we need never 'let a child down' which is something quite different.

So far I have spoken about *adaptation to demands* and the dangers attending this: now I wish to consider *adaption to meet expectations*, which is something very different. (I must make it clear at this point that there is no such distinction in the dictionary, where adaption and adaptation have the same meaning.)

I have referred already to the state of adaption in which a mother exists with her new-born baby (in a supporting element – the environment, father, other family, etc.).

The next stage reached is where a normal mother, deliberately and aware, but without inner stress, is able to meet her baby's needs as it slowly establishes itself as a separate integrated person. The baby's needs will not now necessarily be her own, but she will be so aware of these needs that she will supply them at once with a minimum of delay or hesitation – it will be natural to do this. She does not have to think about this sort of thing, she does it spontaneously, 'with her eyes shut'. The baby, having reached this stage, having had this sort of experience, has expectations and although now and then she will fail to meet them, she will be sufficiently reliable for it to be unnecessary for the baby to *fall back on demands*, which are then *failed expectations*.

If the expectations are met and all goes well, there may still be demands, but the mother may refuse these, more often than not, thus enabling the baby to get angry with her – and it is important for this to be possible.

On the other hand, she will continue to make adaptation to needs, gradually failing as this becomes less necessary. So that eventually there remain only the token adaptations which mothers make to their children's needs even when they are quite grown-up (a special nickname, a kind of hot drink, a funny little joke). Such token adaptations are in addition to those which any mature person makes to the needs of other individuals and of society as a whole.

Now, if things go wrong, which can happen for the many reasons we all know, the resulting history is very different, and produces the kind of child about whom we are so worried.

Because his needs have not been met he has no expectations and can only make demands. What we then have to create is a state of things in which, his needs having been fulfilled, he is, at last, in a position to have expectations. We cannot take such a child back to search for something he has lost, we have to take him forward to discover something he has never known.

So far so good. What are the needs of a baby? Soft breast, warm milk, holding arms and all the rest. How can we hope to provide these things for a tough ten-year-old? And suppose that we *can* produce a fairly satisfactory experience for one child, how can we hope to provide a similar experience for a whole group all apparently with the same needs. Here 'apparently' is the key word. A child said to me recently, 'Fair play wouldn't be any use to people like us, because it would only mean that we'd all get the same thing and each of us needs something different.'

Peter, when he came to us, demanded everything the whole time, and it was important that we should be able to say 'No' to his demands and yet remain concerned about him. (A 'no' without rejection.) He always demanded the *whole* tin of biscuits, *all* our attention – *everything*. He did not, however, allow us to do anything for him, to look after him or comfort him; he had terrible rages, panics and fits of despair – he was never sad, or frightened, or anxious. Gradually he became deeply dependent on one person – a first experience of love, because he had never reached the stage of really loving somebody – and he made it clear to this loved person that she could take care of his nose – his little, helpless nose. Now, up to this point he had been a child with a nose which was always in need of a blow – rather disgusting. A helpless little nose was of course another matter. His grown-up laid in a special stock of handkerchief tissues and took care of Peter's nose. His demands grew less as his expectations became established and gradually he and his grown-up found other ways of feasible caretaking, other practical means of making adaptations to his particular needs.

Another small boy who started by demanding all things bright and beautiful and everything else, settled for a piece of buttered toast each morning – buttered by his therapist at the end of staff breakfast. (For various reasons we have our meals after the children.) This, day after day and month after month.

The important point about such adaptations is that they have to be really possible to make and to continue to make as long as they are necessary – which, after all, is what a mother does, only for us it is a technique to be used in our work while for her it is part of her own private life. Often there is quite a long period during which the child experiments, seeking for something 'which will really work'. It is important that the grown-up should not consent to make an adaptation which cannot be sustained for a period, because reliability is the most important single attribute required in such work. The most essential thing the grown-up can do is to survive, 'to be there in the morning' with something to give, something to take and something to keep for his or herself.

It is interesting to see the understanding that other children show in regard to adaptation to needs (whereas they savagely resent adaption to demands). Recently a child was discussing with me in a group the possibility of a supply of potato crisps to be kept by his therapist so that he could have a packet from time to time. Another child – a newcomer – asked whether everyone would have this, and an experienced member of the group aged about nine explained, 'No, crisps would be right for him; there'll be something you'll find that's right for you, like John who has that special sort of cereal, it really matters to him.'

I have spoken about failure in adaptation having its place in emotional development, and, of course, we are bound – sooner or later – to fail in our adaptations to children's needs. Probably many of you have read some of Dr Winnicott's important papers; he points out the tremendous use which can be made of such failures in the here-and-now situation. It is essential that one should not explain away such failures, but that they should be recognized and acknowledged by grown-up and child, so that the child can at last experience the appropriate anger – the anger which should have been felt in babyhood at the time of the original failure – the time when, as one child said to me recently, 'the wind blew, the bough broke, the cradle fell'.

A child can see astonishing things as failures, and I think this often explains their apparently irrational accusations against the people they love and on whom they depend. The absence of the loved person, whatever the reason and however well prepared the child may be, can be such a failure; or the grown-up's failure to understand something which, anyhow, the child has not said; or understanding something too quickly. It is extraordinary how possible it is for a child going through such an experience with a grown-up to find everything needed in the stuff of everyday existence.

Only when such a failure in adaptation is fully understood by the grown-up and the child, does it become valuable to put it right. What can happen too easily is that the grown-up may feel such a need to make restitution to the child that the failure does not get used.

Quite apart from maintained arrangements there are single adaptations which may be very dramatic.

One such occasion in my own experience was when I took a child out with me, with whom I had a very close bond, and who was extremely dependent upon me at that point. I had to go to Oxford and to do various things in the course of the afternoon, and found myself with no time left to use for something special with James, as I had counted on. We walked up the High Street together, which is very long and usually very crowded; it certainly was on this particular afternoon. I was wondering to myself what I could possibly do that would meet James's needs and be something just for him, when I noticed that he was walking more and more slowly. I was not sure what this was about, so I fortunately did not make any comment, but presently James dropped some distance behind me, and then proceeded up The High at a snail's pace, regardless of jostling crowds and the fact that we were already late.

I decided that he wanted to lose me and find me again, or something like that, so at first I just kept steadily on, although continuing to be aware of his whereabouts. However, when presently he stopped moving altogether and simply stood in the middle of the crowd, I realized that I was not understanding. I threaded my way back to him and waited without saying anything until he started to move again, which he presently did, walking more slowly than I would have believed possible for this particularly agile, lively and independent child. It suddenly dawned on me that this was the means he had found for me to make the necessary adaptation: here was the little child just beginning to walk, whose mother suits her pace to his and is quite prepared to take all the time in the world in order that her child can have the experience of walking by himself, but with the support of her presence. There was a very real problem involved for me in this situation, because I find it extremely hard to walk slowly anyhow, knew we were late and knew also that, unless I could really feel that this was the most important thing for James and for me, however slowly I walked, it would be of no use to him. He didn't even wish to speak (neither of us had said a word about all this) and we were making this long and exhausting journey in absolute silence. I decided that the best hope was for me to notice the architecture in

The High (which normally I don't have time to do), providing that I could still remain concerned with James. This worked very well and made the slow pace more tolerable for me. When we eventually reached the top of the street, James, without comment, suddenly returned to his normal speed and shot down Cornmarket Street like an arrow, but he was extremely happy and contented, and I knew that something important had happened for him, as indeed it had happened for me.

There are certain times when one is especially aware of the necessity of adaptation to individual needs. One such occasion is bedtime; a story read to the whole group, although valuable in other ways, does not fulfil this special purpose and it is difficult to find a way of giving each child an individual experience. Of course this will depend on the particular grown-up and children concerned – everybody has their own special way of doing things, which is the only way that will be satisfactory – personally I rely on what the children call 'mouse parties' and 'perches'.

'Mouse parties' usually mean a bag of sultanas, and the adaptation here consists quite simply in giving a few sultanas to each child. Nothing, however, could be more different than the way in which various children need to receive such a 'mouse party'. One child likes to be given his sultanas one at a time, saying over each sultana, 'That's not much', until suddenly he cries, 'That's enough.' Another child needs to be able to say, 'I don't like sultanas, anyhow.' And the correct response to this is to put his collection of sultanas on the little table by his bed, where he collects it subsequently. Another child holds out his cupped hands into which I must let fall about six sultanas, whereupon he says, 'a little more', and then, 'a little more', and so on until finally he says, 'one more', and that is enough.

There are endless variations and it is important that I remember exactly what each child needs. A fascinating fact is that all the children do get about the same number of sultanas; it is the way in which they receive them which makes the 'mouse party' an individual and special experience.

'Perches' involve my sitting on the side of each bed in turn for a very few minutes; and here again each child uses these few minutes in a special and highly individual way. One child plays a complicated finger game with one of my hands and his own hands. Another child likes me to sing him a French song. Another child always uses this time to tell me something about what he feels it was like inside his mother before he was born. Here again I am often completely amazed by the tremendous use which they make of a few minutes, and I am also very impressed by the respect with which 'perches' are regarded. Children are prepared to wait for their turn and do not interrupt other children's 'perches' if they can help it.

There is another kind of adaptation which I call for convenience 'communication'; this is a valuable means of meeting individual needs in or out of a group – a lifeline between the grown-up and the child.

Communication, again, is something which mothers establish with their babies at quite an early stage, understanding intuitively the deeper inside meaning of what the child is saying and responding in the medium which the child has chosen.

Understanding grown-ups working and playing with children use this kind of communication probably without even noticing that this is what they are doing. Perhaps some of the best work that any of us achieve is that which we understand the least – indeed I think our successes are often more surprising than our failures.

An example of communication was with a boy who had been extremely delinquent, had made a recovery, returned home and was getting on quite well in a state of extreme dependence on his mother. For various reasons he tried to revert to the earlier pattern and found he could no longer be successfully delinquent. He said to me, 'In school a few days ago, I heard a very good poem.' The poem was as follows:

> A centipede was happy quite,
> Until a toad in fun
> Said, 'Pray which leg comes after which?'
> Which sent him into such a pitch
> He lay distracted in a ditch,
> Considering how to run.

I said gravely that I did not think the toad had been in fun at all, that while the centipede was happy he had indeed been running along very fast without his front leg knowing where his back leg was going, and that the toad had, in fact, tried to teach him how to walk. 'Did the centipede', I asked, 'really need to lie kicking in the ditch considering how to run? Had he thought of walking instead?' Edward said that it was mean of the toad to make him think about his feet. I said that I thought it quite fair that the centipede should feel angry with the toad, especially if the centipede started the old running and suddenly found he could not do it any more, just because he knew which foot was which.

Adaptations to needs depend on concern, on therapeutic skill, on having an emotional economy, on being reliable; if to all these you choose to add theoretical knowledge, so much the better, but without the essentials theoretical knowledge is of little use, and of all these essentials reliability seems to be the most important, because it is in your survival that the child will find expectations.

Lately we have come to understand something at the Mulberry Bush which has been of value to us and might be to you. This is a concept of 'concerned neglect'. You will know the feeling of personal guilt which one has when it is impossible to meet the very real needs of one or more children in a group – in fact one is really neglecting them. The important thing is, I think, that both you and the children should realize that this is so, that you *are* neglecting them . . . but at the same time that you are aware of this and continuing to feel concerned about them. We find that this is well worth stating to the children in the actual context of the situation, so that one may say to the child, 'I am terribly sorry. I should be with you and helping you . . . or whatever, and I am not because I am doing something else, but I am going on being worried about you.' No reassuring here, no covering up of one's own personal guilt; this gives the child real assurance of your continued concern for him. I am sure that mothers with big families do this all the time. I often hear people say, 'I cannot imagine how a mother manages with her three or four children, all small, and all needing her at the same time . . .' and I feel that as well as the individual adaptations she makes to each child's needs and meeting of their expectations, there is also this condition of 'concerned neglect' from time to time, which she and they can face and understand and which she is not afraid to state.

Adaption, which I discussed first, will have its moments; there are instants for all of us when we can experience the sense of unity which belongs to the period just after birth; sometimes this will be when we are listening to music, or looking at a beautiful landscape, or experiencing something very deep with somebody else, a grown-up or child. And, in working with children, there will be moments when we are completely involved and it is possible for an instant for child and grown-up to recapture what that earliest experience must have been. What we cannot do is to hold this, to try and maintain it, because this is an illusion and while illusions are terribly valuable they cannot be held and used; they are like the fairy gold which turns into dead leaves.

Adaptation, of course, also creates in some ways an illusion; but there is enough reality for this to be tested, so that it can really be used to help the child to experience something essential which he or she has never known. Perhaps one of the most valuable things we can do for such children is to give them something to lose, since only through loss are they likely to realize experience.

Chapter 22

Need Assessments and Context Profiles

The original Need Assessment was based on the questions which I had come to ask myself when trying to understand an unintegrated disturbed child in the Mulberry Bush School at Standlake, where I worked for many years as therapeutic adviser. The questions on the Need Assessments have always been answered by a group of workers with the subsequent help of the consultant. On the results of the Need Assessment a plan for treatment is then based, depending on the stage of integration reached. Integration in this sense means the achievement of integration into an individual identity, as described in many places by Winnicott.

When Richard Balbernie was invited by the Home Office to take over an approved school to be changed into a therapeutic community, he invited me to become therapeutic adviser there. The primary task of the Cotswold Community has always been the achievement of integration. All boys admitted to the Community have been grossly deprived, are delinquent and deeply disturbed. They usually fall into one of our categories of unintegration.

'Frozen' children
The most primitive of these categories – that is to say, the least integrated – is made up of those whom I have described elsewhere as the 'frozen' children who have suffered interruption of primary experience at the point where they and their mothers would be starting the separating out process, who have been, as it were, broken off rather than separated out from their mothers. They have survived by perpetuating a pseudo-symbiotic state, without

boundaries to personality, merged with their environment and unable to make any real object relationships or to feel the need for them.

Such a child must be provided with the actual emotional experiences of progression to separating out, thereby establishing identity, accepting boundaries and finally reaching a state of dependence on the therapist. This kind of child cannot symbolize what he has never experienced or realized. (A 'frozen' child, on referral, will steal food from the larder because he wants food at that moment and for no other reason. The same child in the course of recovery may steal again from the larder, because his therapist is absent; this stealing will now be symbolic.)

'Archipelago' children

The next category consists of those who have achieved the first steps towards integration, so that one could describe them as made up of ego-islets which have never fused into a continent – a total person. For this reason we call them 'archipelago' children. These children give the impression of being quite mad whenever they are not being quite sane. They are either wildly aggressive, destructive and out of touch in states of panic-rage or terror, or they are gentle, dependent and concerned. They present a bewildering picture till one comes to know them and to understand the meaning of their behaviour. They too need to progress through the process of integration. However, these stormy children are not so difficult to help as are 'frozen' children, because the presence of ego-islets amid the chaos of unassimilated experience makes life more difficult for them. They are, from time to time, very unhappy and aware that they need help. The fact that some primary experiences have been contained and realized results in their having a limited capacity for symbolization, which facilitates communication of a symbolic kind which is not available to 'frozen' ones. Where 'frozen' and 'archipelago' children are concerned, treatment must involve the breakdown or pathological defences, containment of the total child and the achievement of dependence on the therapist as a separate person. These two groups, in which integration has not been sufficient to establish a position from which to regress, are very different from those in the next category.

False selves

Classifying the 'false self' organizations, Winnicott writes:

> At one extreme: the false self sets up as real and it is this that observers tend to think is the real person. In living relationships, work relationships, and friendships, however, the false self begins to fail. In situations in which what is expected is a whole person the false self has some essential lacking. At this extreme the true self is hidden. (Winnicott, 1960, pp. 142–3)

Caretaker selves

Having described other types of false selves advancing towards health, Winnicott continues: 'Still further towards health: the false self is built of identifications'. This form of organization he has described as the 'caretaker self' (Winnicott, 1960). The elaborate defence takes various forms and is often difficult to recognize, especially because the 'little self' part of the child is carefully concealed by the caretaker (for example, there may be a delinquent 'caretaker' which steals without conflict, on behalf of the 'little self').

There are also other, occasional syndromes:

Burnt-out autism

A child who has been at an earlier stage in an autistic state, but is now gradually recovering.

Psychotic pocket

A child who, while otherwise relatively functioning though often delinquent, has a psychotic part of himself, of which he is quite unaware, but which breaks through into his consciousness from time to time.

Let us now consider the four categories which are the most usual to find on referral and their treatment.

Frozen children

These need to reach depression (usually very deep). This is the most delinquent group. The depression is followed by dependence on one person. In communication with this person he will need to learn the nature of delinquency and its cause, his severe early deprivation. He will also need to learn that delinquency is a form of addiction, which could be described as self-provision accompanied by intense excitement; it is to this excitement that the boy becomes addicted, and the depression which he reaches through dependence has much in common with withdrawal symptoms.

These realizations put him on the road to recovery and ego functioning, aided by deep concern and care, with adaptations made to his needs (which are primary). These adaptations may be needed for some time and are essentially symbolic, very often taking the form of a special food or drink, given by the boy's therapist at regular times.

Periods of communication alone with the therapist are also essential. The initial aim of such periods is to encourage children to communicate anything, however trivial, and to meet this with response and encouragement. Gradually this important exchange will develop quite naturally into discussion about the boy and his feelings and through such discussion he can gain insight.

Archipelago children

As has been pointed out in the description of archipelago children, they have not integrated to a state from which they can regress. The task of the therapist, therefore, is to build bridges of experience between the islets of ego. This can be achieved by one therapist with devoted care over a long period. It will be possible for him to point out to the child in the sea of unintegration that there *is* an islet he can reach. Boy and adult will both tend to talk of this in symbolic terms. Indeed the boy will often introduce the island theme and may make an archipelago out of clay or Plasticine to describe his state. The vital need in the treatment of an archipelago child is to maintain contact with voice and wherever possible by touch. The terrible panics become briefer and the boy is increasingly able to use the bridges of good experience (food, communication and symbolic play). At the same time he develops a deep and trusting relationship with his therapist. His recovery may be quite quick, but sometimes he goes through a short period as a caretaker self before fully integrating.

False self children

These are children who through primary deprivation have only a tiny real self contained by a shell of adaption to demands. The first task is to penetrate the façade, through communication and adaptation to needs, the aim being to achieve a regression, at which point the false self ceases functioning and the therapist takes over the little real self, which at this point may be quite helpless, even speechless or incontinent. The regression does not last for long but needs the kind of maternal preoccupation to be seen so clearly with normal babies and their mothers; from this state the boy will recover into a normal state of integration.

Caretaker selves

This is the most nearly integrated group of unintegrated children. The syndrome is formed towards the end of the first year, when due to lack of maternal love and preoccupation one part of the child takes over the other part of himself and assumes a maternal role, although one which is somewhat strict and inhibiting. Treatment as with a false self child involves the caretaker part handing over the little real self to the therapist, when there will be a regression.

This regression can take many forms; I have known a child stay in bed for several weeks and need to be fed and treated like a baby. Recovery is from one moment till the next providing the therapist is devoted and reliable.

The occasional syndromes which I have mentioned, 'burnt-out autism' and the 'psychotic pocket', are very rare. Burnt-out autism is characteristic of a child who *has* been autistic and keeps some of the characteristics of the autistic child. It is important that he should be treated as a normal person; that he is reasoned with and encouraged. Delinquency can be explained to him as an addiction – if indeed he is delinquent, which is uncommon. Above all, firm solid relationships should be established to function in every way, with affection and kindness but also firmness. He will often communicate through play with small toys.

I have tried to indicate the kind of treatments needed by the different categories of unintegrated children based on Need Assessments, but these are merely indications. Each child is unique, and I can only sketch in the sort of treatment required; in every case it needs to be specially for this child. The most important matter is the steady loving care which such a child needs. Always it must be remembered that this boy has had a tragic babyhood and childhood, which it is our task to replace by the provision of primary experience.

Assessment of needs of the unintegrated
NAME – *Adam*   DATE – 22 September 1985

   a   Does this boy panic (a state of unthinkable anxiety)?

Yes. Can explode violently. This is much less frequent. Recently panicked briefly on Tim's day off. Chris needed to hold him. Chris feels there is something in the dynamic between Adam and himself which may precipitate panic. Adam is much more contained with Tim who has not seen him panic for a couple of months.

Mrs Drysdale – Felt panic could be manifested as a tantrum, rage, despair or physical symptoms, e.g. epilepsy may be linked with panic. Panic could be distinguished from rage as the person is unable to act consciously, cannot be reached or make contact. The anxiety is unthinkable, cannot be contained, the person is *in* a panic.

The nature and source of panic could be described and explained to Adam in simple terms: something dreadful happened to him when very young, before he was able to cope with it and his response had been to panic. Now when things are too much he still panics. The use of the ordinary word 'panic' can help fix the experience and make it conscious. He must know that adults understand and can contain panic and that it is not inevitable, that he can be helped by anticipation and support. Some children can use the idea of a special signal or password to indicate the approach of panic. When given, this signal must always be taken seriously (as must any suicidal threat) and the child given one-to-one attention as a priority. This need not take much time.

   b   Does he disrupt (break in on a group happening or activity)?

When Adam's frustration explodes, he impinges on others. Under stress he can create a wild, excited and violent atmosphere doing 'stunts'. At bedtimes, usually when Tim is away, his extreme and noisy restlessness can become provocative – often draws reactions from Simon and Brett (both of whom Chris looks after). Adam does not directly break into group or individual activities.

Mrs Drysdale – Disruption must be interrupted at once. Explain to the child what he is doing and that ultimately he will be the one to suffer most from disrupting others. We should *never* get used to boys' symptoms.

Adam's restlessness at bedtime could be helped by special provision of something he liked and could do only while in bed. An example of a girl who dealt with frustration of waiting for buses by keeping a good book to read only on these occasions. Also a delinquent boy who could ask adults for a special sweet when the need for excitement began to build up (he now flies a kite which goes up and up while he stays on the ground).

From this information, is this boy integrated as a person or is he unintegrated?

If integrated, proceed to assess this boy's needs.

If unintegrated, then further classification is needed in order to determine the stage of integration reached (see questions 1–4 below).

Further classification of the unintegrated boy

1 What is the syndrome of deprivation? This is judged by the degree of ego functioning which can be assessed by the state of feeling of this boy in regard to:

   a Personal guilt (refers to concern and a guilt which accepts personal responsibility for harm done to others and which can lead to reparation, as opposed to pathological guilt).

Increasing signs of this; will now clear up spillages spontaneously. In a group will be the one to acknowledge his part in dubious activities, e.g. recently he and John were pushing Ted on a go-kart in a dangerous way. John denied it but

Adam admitted that he had ignored Ted's call to stop. Can take a moral stance.

b Is he or has he been dependent on people or a person?

There is an attachment to Tim and sense in him of missing something when Tim is away. Tim feels Adam uses the adults and structure of the household as a whole. Adam trusts Tim to meet regressed needs, e.g. make clothes for his gollies. Receives adaptation twice a week at bedtime.

c Does he unconsciously merge with another or a group?

When bored or frustrated may seek exciting pairing – particularly with Brett. Attempts to merge with Chris – more subtly now – and male visitors whom he compares with *Star Wars* actor Harrison Ford.

Mrs Drysdale – Adam's wish to merge with a male adult. There would be a part of the adult wanting to merge with the boy. Adults must be concerned and kind but not become part of him. Warn adults, e.g. visitors, of this tendency in him. Always interrupt and anticipate, e.g. warn Adam to 'keep his edge'. Need to merge is an element of a frozen child. We can speak to him of being separated from his mother at a crucial time, e.g. weaning, and wanting to join on to someone ever since. A child usually feels itself separate from its mother by the end of the first year.

Patricia asked about the moral stance Adam often takes and its relationship to his upbringing. His adoptive parents, in contrast to one's expectations of a minister and his wife, take a *laissez-faire* line, perhaps wanting to be good objects.

Mrs Drysdale – this must be raised with the parents. Their permissiveness will not help Adam.

d Does he show empathy in what he says or does (capacity to imagine what it feels like to be in someone else's shoes while remaining in one's own)?

Has an acute sensitivity to others' states of mind which he can use to advantage. He may attempt to 'psych' people by expounding on their motives or analysing their responses, making them uncomfortable. He can also express empathic understanding. Moral overtones often suggest a defensive detachment.

    e   Stress (how he deals with such feelings).

Becomes noisy, crashes around clumsily, looks wild and does aggressive 'stunts', has destructive 'accidents'. Can smoulder, sitting very tense and still, with a concentrated look of hatred/anger. Food and drink can help if offered in time. He will search for extra food when restless.

Mrs Drysdale – We must always interrupt. Tell him to sit down quietly for a moment and 'get back inside himself'.

Patricia was concerned about repressing disturbance.

Mrs Drysdale – interrupting behaviour designed to create excitement will uncover feelings which a child should not be left with alone. Can offer food or drink at such times to redirect him. Show anger can be expressed verbally without a great deal of noise and shouting. Adults by example can demonstrate how anger can be real but expressed in a contained way.

    f   Communication (Does he really communicate or does he chatter in a stereotyped way? Does he use non-verbal communication?)

Yes. Can communicate directly. Also uses his gollies who have different voices for characters and interact differently with individuals. Not using drawing much at present though this has been important.

    g   Identification (Does he seem to model himself, as distinct from merger, on another person he admires?)

More ready to merge than identify. Fascination with Harrison Ford (see above).

    h   Depression (Is he sometimes depressed, indifferent, or always apparently cheerful? Is he at times deeply sad or in a state of 'hibernation'? Does he act out in a depression?)

Has brief moments of sadness. Often paranoid overtones.

Spends moments, particularly in school, quite shut off – usually, however, more in anger perhaps than sadness, when there is no one to help immediately with a particular difficulty.

Mrs Drysdale – important to recognize, empathize and support, but not relieve depression in Adam; say, 'You are feeling awful, I am so sorry, would you like to go to bed?' Explain that everyone needs to be able to feel sad at times in their life. His sense of being alone does need relief, e.g. when he speaks of being found dead in the morning, his fear is of depression overtaking him when he is vulnerable in his sleep – reassure him that people are around, leave a night light on and his door open.

Sheila – shows much less manic cheerfulness.

Mrs Drysdale – It will help to comment on changes in him and the progress he has made.

i Aggression (verbal or physical; direct or indirect)

Little direct aggression towards adults. Mutters obscenities, can shout and swear. Crashes about. Attacks his 'stuntman' figure. Other boys complain of his roughness (he is very large for his age) though bullying rarely witnessed by adults.

Mrs Drysdale – Adam uses a small model man whom he subjects to dreadful accidents in the guise of 'stunts'. This was felt to be a self-object. Mrs Drysdale thought it vital to have a sense of what his fantasy was about: his real parents. We could work hard to create an edifice over a great vacuum if who he was and where he came from was not opened up. Need to find this out and how much he is aware of. Approach with sensitivity at appropriate moments and give him opportunities to ask questions. Explain that his real parents were not able to care for him, rather than let him think there was fault in himself.

2 What is his capacity for play?

a Does he play a lot alone with pleasure? (narcissistic)
b Does he make use of a transitional object? (transitional)

c Does he usually like to play with one other, usually a grown–up? (pre–oedipal)

d Does he play with more than one grown–up at a time? (oedipal)

e Does he play with other boys and is he able to keep to rules? (post–oedipal)

a Plays alone a lot often around stage or film sets. Progress towards constructive rather than destructive play. Elements of sadism in play with his little stuntman figure.

b Three gollies (see communication) – they are from 'The Nursery' – a place in the past, outside time. They return to Toyland at night when they come alive.

c No – wants grown–ups to give help and attention, constructing elaborate sets. Some word play.

d On occasions in word play. A quick and dry sense of humour.

e Yes, he can. Enjoys football but not indoor games.

3 What is his capacity for learning? (Does he learn from experience in every sort of learning situation?)

Potentially good capacity to learn. Can talk interestingly and with insight on various subjects which suggests he can retain and use information well. Spends a great deal of time constructing film sets. His feelings have improved but he is hampered by very poor co–ordination.

4 What is his capacity for self preservation? (Does he take care of and value himself or symbols of himself? Does he invite attack or make suicidal gestures?)

Does not invite attack. Poor co–ordination and clumsiness results in bumps and cuts. Wants and enjoys care and attention. Somewhat fearful of germs, parasites, etc., following ringworm infestation. Stuntman (self–object) receives hard treatment – almost torture.

From this information, it should be possible to assess the stage of integration reached.

Mrs Drysdale – The Need Assessment suggested Adam was

'*recovering frozen*'. He needs as much individual care as possible to build up the missing parts of himself. Adaptations are very important in this.

The main indicators for this conclusion were the presence of panic, disruption and merger and the frequent use of excitement to compensate for lack of contentment.

Context Profiles

Every now and then we need to examine a child in detail. He may by now be established in the Community, but we want to know more about him – for example, should he move on to the next household? Such a child is studied for a week by the whole household. Each person records in detail any experience he has had with the boy. We do not admit detached observations into this kind of study, for we need each person's total response to the child, which will be both objective and subjective together. Winnicott once described this by saying in conversation that 'For a moment we see the whole child, with all the bits brought together.'

The Profile is then arranged in terms of time of day, and subsequently discussed with the consultant. I can only illustrate with one Profile here, but I hope this will give some idea of the value of the approach.

A Context Profile
Monday 14 May 1984
(John spent yesterday in the Brecon Beacons, hill-walking, with a small group from the Cottage).

7.40 a.m.
John was under his duvet, fast asleep with his thumb in his mouth. I put my hand on his shoulder and gently shook, 'John'.

He groaned and turned over, still under his duvet. 'Who is it?'

'It's Carmel, good morning'.

'Hullo, I'm tired', a nose appearing. He groaned and put out his hand which I took.

'I was asleep before ten o'clock last night', he said with his thumb still in his mouth.

'Yes, you were very very tired. Would you like a cup of coffee – and I'll get you Andy's note?'

'Yes', he said and he scratched his head with my hand.

CARMEL

7.50 a.m.

I returned with a cup of coffee and a note from Andy. I touched his shoulder – John – 'You again.'

Carmel – 'Yes it's me again. Here is your coffee and a note from Andy.'

John (sucking his thumb and squealing) – 'Aaagh, Andy, read it to me.'

I read quite a funny note. When I finished John squealed and again put out his hand for me to hold.

John – 'Did you see him yesterday? Did you come to see if I was here?'

Carmel – 'Sort of. But I knew you had gone to Wales.'

John – 'I nearly didn't go. I was too sleepy and it was too early.'

Carmel – 'Well take your time. You have a few minutes before it's time to get up.'

He snuggled under his duvet.

CARMEL

8.05 a.m.

I returned to John's room and told him it was time to get up. He said, 'You again!' and half played with a grumpy voice. I helped him out of bed, holding his hands, and he swung around so that he was standing up. He got dressed very quickly after he watched me choosing some clothes. While I was outside and his door was closed he grumbled half to himself and half to me. He wasn't getting up, no, he wasn't going to get dressed, he didn't have any toothpaste because he had lost it. We then went down for his wash.

In the bathroom he washed himself. I asked him where his nice new sponge was and he said he had left it at home. 'I hate these sort of washes', he said filling the sink with water. He washed his face with his hands and when he got toothpaste on his hands too, he said, 'Look what I mean, messy a second time'. During his wash he was quite grumpy, but half joking to himself. On his way back down to his room he passed Tony in the kitchen and, looking at him out of the corner of his eye, said, 'Look at Tony, reckon he's not knackered'; everyone laughed at this and so John joined in.

I brushed his hair in his room. On the way back down the corridor he laughed at me and said 'Look at the way you walk, Carmel' and he mimicked me.

CARMEL

8.10 a.m.

I was telling Nigel not to play with his skateboard in the corridor, outside his room. John called out from his room, 'Shut up Brian, you're not the manager now.' I went into his room and pointed out that whether I was the manager or not Nigel shouldn't do this.

'You're not the manager', he repeated.

BRIAN

8.15 a.m.

While cooking breakfast I gave John a photo from yesterday's paper of the Manchester United game. We talked about his 'team', the players in the picture and various trainers. It was quite an interesting conversation and then John tried to trick Tony by telling him that Manchester United won 7–1, and winking at me to get me to play along.

NIGEL

8.15 a.m.

John came into the kitchen, looking mischievous – I said 'You caught the sun on your nose yesterday, John' – he said 'Yeah I can feel it' and grinned, then said 'Jack the lad – you're Jack the lad' as he walked out. He didn't explain and I don't know what he meant by it.

TONY

8.20 a.m.

John managed breakfast quite well, passing things to me, i.e. cereal and teapot when I asked for them. He also tested Tony's toasted egg sandwiches for me. I noticed that he ate his boiled egg by peeling away the white and eating the yolk separately. Towards the end of the meal Edward was getting into a state and John was affected by this, becoming quite excited.

NIGEL

8.25 a.m.

Over breakfast I tried to engage John in conversation about our trip to the Brecon Beacons yesterday. He wasn't very forthcoming and it took several attempts for him to join in. He talked briefly and said 'It was very windy' – he seemed to be missing Andy a lot, and I was seated in the place Andy normally has.

TONY

8.45 a.m.

John brought some news into the morning meeting about Norman Whiteside, a Manchester United player. He waited until the end of the meeting and seemed very self-conscious, spoke quietly and was unsure of himself.

TONY

8.50 a.m.

We met in the sitting-room. John asked to sit next to me. Keith was sitting on my other side and as usual I gave Keith a chewy sweet for during the meeting. John put his hands over his eyes (as he usually does) and then asked, 'Is it over?' He giggled a couple of times during the meeting and towards the end volunteered some news about Manchester United football club – quite seriously.

After the meeting we went to tidy John's room. On the way there, John said to me, 'I hate you because you hate me.' I asked him if he was missing Andy and he replied, 'I wish Andy were here, he wants to hear about my news, about Penny Fann.' We tidied John's room and he then showed which football player he had talked about in the meeting – a very young seventeen-year-old who was 'no good now'.

CARMEL

9.05 a.m.

John called out to me 'I've got to park my car in the car park' and walked out of the house without waiting for a reply. I was putting my shoes on and explained it wasn't quite time for Poly yet. He said, 'Yeah, but I've got to get it.' He went out to his go-kart and came in a few minutes later.

TONY

9.10 a.m.
While I was in the kitchen John came out of the sitting-room after having messed around on the piano. He came up to me and pretended to have a fight with me and then swore quite loudly as he walked off down the corridor to his room.

NIGEL

9.10 a.m.
I was with Keith making his bed and he was making a lot of noise. John came past singing and generally high. 'Shut up – I'll smash your face in.'

I was making no contact with him and he called this out as he passed the door.

BRIAN

9.15 a.m.
I walked over to Poly with John and Keith. John was very agitated and noisy. He walked ahead of us, and when we got to the little bridge by the fish pond he stopped and assembled his go-kart at the top of the hump. He took a long time. I went back to wait for him. He was agitated, grumbling to himself, half laughing. I picked up the rope and front two wheels, saying 'I'll drive this bit and you drive the rest.'

He shouted 'Hey' and laughed, coming after me pulling the last two wheels.

He asked me to help him carry his go-kart upstairs to the Poly area. By now he was again very noisy, and getting quite out of touch. I took hold of his wrist firmly and I asked him if he could feel my hand. John said he could and I said it seemed he was tired and also missing Andy, but he had planned to do a number of things in Poly and would need to be able to concentrate. He squealed and said yes. A few minutes later he made to follow me out of the area to my meeting. I told him to stop his nonsense and he then decided he would wave from the window instead.

CARMEL

9.20 a.m.
I was in Poly and he walked past shouting 'Shut up four eyes' and tapped me on the shoulder. He laughed and smiled, then walked off. I asked him why he did this – no reply.

BRIAN

10.30 a.m.

I took toast up to Poly, this time it was brown bread. John realized this and exclaimed, 'Bloody hell, what no bread!' I returned to the Cottage. Then I forgot to ask Tony about an outstanding float. Tony talked about having given £10 to Carmel. As I was leaving John said, 'You will have to give me the £10' – he laughed. Then he called out 'You're visiting me tonight' with a smile on his face. In fact Andy comes in at 1.30 and this will not be the case.

BRIAN

Poly

John wanted to work on his go-kart as soon as he came into the education area and didn't accept that he could do it later in the morning, after tea-break (usually an accepted boundary). He was quite agitated so I spent ten minutes or so with him, working out the next stages. He settled down, accepted that he should do it later and then sat down at his desk to write a letter to Andy about his walking trip yesterday. He spent about forty-five minutes writing the letter then drew a picture of the hills, the route we had taken and some of the things we had seen. He showed me the letter and drawing – obviously satisfied with them – and then had his reading time with Ann. After tea-break he worked on his go-kart with Jim through until twelve. He was absorbed and involved in making large staples out of nails, sanding down the go-kart and preparing to paint it.

TONY

12.10 p.m.

John was quite difficult at the table and didn't make much positive contact with anyone. He was very noisy and provocative, refusing to listen to simple requests to be quieter, not shout to the far end of the table. As at breakfast, Andy's absence seemed very important. He complained about his piece of chicken, refused to eat it because it smelled funny (it seemed OK in fact). He laughed in a high, excited way, said he wanted another one. Very abusive to me when I said his piece seemed OK, perhaps he could have one of the spares when we came to share out second helpings. He demanded his potatoes very roughly, spoke to me all through the meal in a very belligerent manner, except for a few seconds near the end of the meal when he rested on my arm and said 'I'm sorry'. I asked if he was missing Andy and said that it was all right if he felt bad. He didn't answer and the rest of the meal carried on as before, John half helping to give out the pudding but causing difficulties at the same time. He was extremely hard work to be next to and nearly all of the attempts I made to bring him into a positive conversation failed/were ignored. He ate quite a few potatoes but refused the chicken when the extra food was given out – several pieces of chicken were uneaten which he could have had.

TONY

12.45 p.m.
After lunch I had to remove the sleeping-in mattress from Graham's room. As I was doing it John came along the corridor and said 'Who's messing around with the fucking mattress?'

NIGEL

12.55 p.m.
Before talking groups John was in the sitting-room lying on some cushions. George tried to take a cushion and John became very aggressive towards him so I had to intervene. As a result John became aggressive towards me and started swearing at me.

NIGEL

1.05 p.m.
Talking groups – the boys were ready when I joined them having been held up. They were all calling each other names and swearing. Things calmed down for a while and John talked about when he did his 12+. He said if you had 99 out of 100 you went to a posh school but when he went into his exam he didn't have a clue about any of it and had to make up all the answers. He giggled a great deal and swore a lot. I told him he couldn't talk like that in talking group. A large proportion of the disturbance in the group was between John and Keith. I felt John should leave the room and asked him to do so. He said he wouldn't, and after I suggested that he may have to be moved he got up and moved towards the partition – he said there was one thing he was going to do before he went out, and grabbed Keith, it seemed, round the neck and tried to punch him in

the face. He was taken out by Tony in the midst of what could be described as a brawl.

PHILIPPA

1.15 p.m.

After John had left the talking group and sat in his room with Tony for a while, he then went back to dining-room and threatened George saying he was going to beat him up. I had to carry him down to his room and hold him for a short period. During this he struggled quite a lot and told me that I was not strong enough to control him. After a while I thought he had relaxed enough for me to release him. He lay on his bed for a while and then tipped over his shelf, knocking his things on the floor and also took a few pictures off the wall. I told him that he should clear up the mess he had made, which at first he was reluctant to do. He then started talking about what had happened in the talking group in a rather excited and incoherent manner. It emerged that he had been antagonistic towards George and a struggle had started which Keith also got caught up in. He told me how he had held George's hand and threatened to hit him. He also said he could easily take on two people with his own 'two hands', though he thought it was a bit unfair. After this he said he wanted to go to Poly but I said perhaps he should wait a while. This seemed to spur him into picking up the things he had knocked onto the floor. Soon afterwards Carmel came in and asked if I would walk over to the Poly with John. He rushed over and was first to arrive, going straight in as Ann was already there.

NIGEL

1.15 p.m.

John was asked to leave his talking group and started a fight as he left. I had to hold him for a while before we went down to his room. He was incensed by George and both were trying to fight each other very hard. In his room he shouted and swore saying he wasn't frightened of George etc., he would get him back, take him on for a fight later. He started to calm down a little when I pointed out how difficult his day had been at various points – suggested he might be worried about something. He immediately denied anything was wrong and when I suggested it again, pointing out that he seemed to be finding a number of situations quite difficult, he became noisy and abusive. I said I could imagine him missing Andy, thinking about his missed meeting with Carmel yesterday, thinking about the coming break and feeling pretty mixed up about them all. This seemed to make a slight difference and he settled a little.

TONY

1.30 –2.00 p.m.

Edward did not get into Poly but was lying on the grass in Poly square. Brian was with him encouraging him to get up and return to the Cottage. I went over to talk to them. John, who normally waits and waves from the Poly window began shouting at Edward, encouraging him to stay where he was. I then walked back to the Cottage; a few minutes later Nigel and Brian were helping to carry Edward across the Spinney. John came running into the garden and tried pulling people off Edward. I went outside and was very angry with him. He was agitated but seemed in control and not merged with Edward. I caught him glancing towards main square and realized he was waiting for Andy. I said I felt it was on purpose so Andy would find him messing about and take him inside; I said that Andy had a meeting now and would not be able to do this. John half listened, half ready to run and with intermittent swearing at me. I told him to go back to Poly where he had things to get on with. At this point Andy came into the Spinney, and I went to explain to him. Andy told him to go back to Poly and we went inside.

I was washing up and John capered about outside, provoking for physical management. He banged at the window by the sink. I made a blubbering noise and told him he was acting a bit like a baby demanding attention, and that nobody was going to drag him inside. He banged on the window harder, swearing at me, and pretended to smash the window with a stick. I told him Andy would see him later and that he should go back to Poly. He ran off then.

CARMEL

1.40 p.m.

When I came in to work John was in the garden having a very loud argument with Carmel. When I appeared he started swearing and shouting at me and obviously wanted me to get into a big thing with him. I said he ought to be in Poly and that I'd see him at 4.30. He capered about shouting and swearing and I went into the office to do some work. He carried on making a lot of noise for a while, then went over to Poly.

ANDY

1.50 p.m.
I left the Cottage to take the car back to the car park. John came and grabbed the car as I set off. I had to stop driving, he was swearing and banging on the car roof. I was really angry with him and told him to get stuffed – in the end I left the car in the middle of the road and walked away from him. I went out five minutes later and got into the car – he was sitting by the swimming pool sucking his thumb – again he ran over and stood in front of the car but he wasn't quick enough and just stood swearing after me. I think he thought I was going to run him over.

PHILIPPA

3.30 p.m.
I went into Poly to tell Tony about a transport meeting. John came over to me with Tony. Tony asked him to get on with something. John said, 'Fucking bitch . . . you wait for me for once . . . I have to wait for my meetings.' He moved away after this.

CARMEL

4.30 p.m.
When I went up to Poly John shouted, 'There's the Japanese bitch, Indian bitch, old cow – you tried to run me over' – when we got back to the house he continued to be provocative especially about me sitting near him.

PHILIPPA

4.30 –4.45 p.m.
Most people were in the sitting-room to have a cup of tea. John fairly quiet, lounging on the sofa, but very bossy and nasty about everything he said – 'Give me a cup of tea then' and so on. I said that there didn't seem much point him sitting with everyone if he just wanted to be awful. He didn't say much after that.

ANDY

Poly afternoon

John was badly affected by some disturbance outside the Poly at the start of the afternoon, ran out and went back to the Cottage. When he came in he wanted to get into painting his go-kart immediately and we had a difficult time in trying to establish what needed to be done first. After ten minutes or so he eventually accepted that the kart needed finishing properly and we worked together to complete the sanding. The painting went very well, John accepted the basic boundaries – how to make sure the paint didn't get on the floor, etc., and was thoughtful about what he was doing. He spent the rest of the afternoon doing things to get it ready, sawed pieces of wood for the axle supports and cleared up all his things at 4.00 in a very straightforward way. He looked for a lot of support and contact from me, and spent a lot of time with George asking for advice. John spent the last half-hour playing with the toy soldiers on his own, quite contained. He was 'lost' in his own inner world, playing out the game he often gets into – soldiers fighting with John going into details of their talk, playing the part of all the soldiers. He made all the noises when they hit each other, focusing on how they all were getting their own back, coming alive and fighting. This play is quite repetitive though less frequent than previously – quite a useful outlet for him.

TONY

5.45 p.m.

I announced a new arrangement for the seating at the dining-table. John got very cross about it and started swearing and shouting at me. I said that I thought he was very angry with me and that we could talk about it in his room. John got even louder then and I took him out of the sitting-room down to his bedroom. He was still complaining about his place at the table and saying he wasn't going to sit there. I said that in that case he needn't come to the meal. He carried on swearing about this and I told him that I would talk about things with him but that I wasn't prepared just to listen to a load of abuse. I left him then.

ANDY

6.00 p.m.

As we were about to start tea John appeared in the kitchen and again started swearing at me. I took him to his room again and held him briefly as he was trying to kick me. He said I was trying to break his arm and I said I wasn't hurting him at all but wasn't going to let him hurt me either. After a couple of minutes I let go of him. He said he was going to wreck his room and I told him he wasn't. I tried a couple of times to call another man as I felt I should be with the group at the meal, rather than with John, but this obviously went unheard.

John was obviously very distressed, abusing me, but also half crying. I said that I thought he was upset and angry with me and that he should tell me about it straightforwardly as I knew he could. He said he wouldn't, and again threatened to wreck his room. I said I'd ask Nigel to come and sit with him. He said he'd punch his head in and I told him he wouldn't. I started walking off to get Nigel, and John said he'd lock himself in the loo. I said 'OK, go on then.' He then said, 'I'll hold my door shut.' I said 'OK' and he went into his room and shut the door.

ANDY

6.40 p.m.

After tea I went to see how John was. He was in his bed with the duvet over his head. I said we were going to have a meeting and did he want to come. He said no. I said that sometime in the evening I'd like to sit down with him and have a cup of tea or coffee and hear all about the trip to Wales. He said he wanted to do that.

I spent a lot of the evening washing up. He came in at various times and said, 'We're all in heaven you know' or 'This is heaven'.

ANDY

7.00 –7.20 p.m. – Meeting

At 6.55 I went down to John's room to tell him I was about to meet him. This meeting was postponed from yesterday, when he went on a climbing trip to Wales. His door was shut and he was lying in bed, rocking under his duvet. His record-player was on quite loud. In a corner by his bed was a pile of scraps of paper – he had torn up his note from Andy. I said that I was going to meet him in a few minutes after I had cooked his beefburger. I suggested he tidy his room a bit – I returned with a dustpan and brush.

Five minutes later I came down to start his meeting. He was still in bed, record-player on and the dustpan where I had placed it. I asked John if I could turn off his record-player and he said yes.

I sat down in my usual place. There was a few minutes' silence – John was under his duvet.

John – 'I'm dying . . . of cancer . . . I have a bad pain in my stomach.'

Carmel – 'What sort of pain . . . have you had it a long time?'

John – 'A sharp pain . . . I'm going to die.'

He spent the next five minutes talking quietly to himself under his duvet, about death and dying.

At one point I said that people had pains for a number of different reasons apart from cancer.

For another five minutes he got quieter and more still and eventually slid off his bed on to the floor. He then went under his bed.

John – 'Oh heaven . . . I hear voices outside . . . it's Graham.'

He looked at the things under his bed and in a quiet voice reported on what he found and what he could hear. He was dead and now in heaven and was watching everything. I said 'Hallo' a number of times. He wondered if I could be in heaven too but said I was on earth, probably celebrating John's death, even saying he should have died earlier. At one point he said 'Well, I did smoke.' (I felt it important not to comment or play into his feeling I wanted him dead. It seemed a projection of the fury towards the two parent figures, Andy and myself. Such an interpretation would only increase a sense of paranoia).

However, with five minutes to go I said – 'Hallo John, it's five minutes to the end. I would like to know if there is anything I could do to help you?' He encouraged me then to continue calling hallo, by making as if to search for my voice. I eventually called hallo and gave his duvet a gentle rock as I do when I wake him, talking to him as if he was asleep. He wanted to remain dead and in heaven. He called to God and wrote a note – 'Thank God' which he gave to me. I then called, 'Hallo, it's the end of your meeting.' He wrote me a little note which said 'The End of John'. I replied again, 'The end of the meeting – goodbye.' He followed me complaining of his tummy. I said he should have a hot-water bottle. He said he didn't want to go to bed and went to look for Andy.

CARMEL

7.30 –8.00 p.m.

I asked John if he wanted to go for a walk with binoculars down to the lake with Jeffrey and Graham. During the whole of the walk he kept on using the binoculars to explore his environment. Any bird he saw he asked me about, 'What's that bird?' John became annoyed when Graham fooled about but seemed to tolerate him.

Both Jeffrey and John looked at things together. When we got to the lake we saw a Red Crested Pochard and I told him this. While walking back Jeffrey tried running through a list of the birds we had seen; John tried to remember the Red Crested Pochard but could not quite get the name right. John was constantly experimenting with the binoculars and asking questions.

BRIAN

8.20 p.m.

I sat down with John at the table. We had a cup of coffee and chatted about his walk. He told me about where they'd walked and what they'd done. Then he got a piece of paper with the story of the walk which he'd written in Poly. He gave it to me and said he'd drawn a picture too but had left it in Poly.

ANDY

8.25 p.m.

I had to say that John could not use the Cottage tape-recorder tonight because Jeffrey had not used it last night. He just said 'OK' when I told him and made no fuss – he was talking with Andy.

BRIAN

8.40 p.m.

John very friendly during his wash. He was a bit cross because he'd lost his toothpaste but Carmel found it and gave it to him and he was quite pleased.

ANDY

9.15 p.m.

In his visit John had Weetabix with hot milk and banana milk-shake as usual. When I came in he said, 'You're going to finish reading the book tonight.' I said, 'No, I think there's still a few chapters left.' (The book is *Emil and the Detectives*).

Then he said, 'I wore your woolly hat yesterday.' I asked which one and he told me, then he said 'Steve wore your ski hat and your gloves and your scarf. I wanted them 'cos I only had your hat.' I said, 'Did it keep you warm?' 'Yes.'

I then picked up the book which was broken in two. I commented on this and John said, 'I didn't break it. I think it must have fallen on the floor, I'll sellotape it together tomorrow.' I said that would be good.

I then read a chapter of the book which John is listening to with pleasure and then finished the visit.

ANDY

9.45 p.m.

I said goodnight to John at about 9.45 – he was playing at being a disc jockey in his room using his record-player and singles. He seemed quite oblivious to anything else happening around him though he did acknowledge my presence.

NIGEL

9.45 p.m.

I was talking to Nigel when I heard John talking in his room next to his record-player. He was introducing a record as if he was a DJ. When he realized that I was listening he grinned and dived under his bedclothes.

'Is this Radio Watts?' I asked.

'Yes,' he replied with a smile.

I walked away.

BRIAN

10.00 p.m.

I went to say goodnight to John. His nightlight was behind the curtains and when I switched it on he decided that it looked nice there so I left it there. I tucked his duvet round him a bit and he held on to one of my hands briefly. We said goodnight to each other and I went out.

ANDY

10.02 p.m.

I left Edward's room, opposite John's, and he called me to say goodnight. I went in and he held out his hands. I took them and he said, 'I was stupid today wasn't I, about the car.' I told him that what he had done was dangerous and that he could have been hurt. He said he was sorry about today and would have a better day tomorrow.

PHILIPPA

10.15 p.m.
I went in as usual to say goodnight to John.

John – 'Can you pluck my pillows?'

I usually say 'Shall I fluff your pillows up?'

I made the noise of a hen and he said, 'Pluck, like a chicken.'

I turned his duvet over and he squealed and stretched out his hand.

We said goodnight.

CARMEL

Bibliography

Place of publication is London unless otherwise stated.

Ardrey, R. (1967) *The Territorial Imperative*. Collins.

Bain, A. and Barnett L. (1986) *The Design of a Day Care System in a Nursery Setting for Children under Five*. Tavistock Institute of Human Relations Occasional Paper no. 8.

Balbernie, R. (1966) *Residential Work with Children*. Human Context Books.

Bettelheim, B. (1950) *Love Is Not Enough*. New York: Free Press.

Dockar-Drysdale, B. (1968) *Therapy in Child Care*. Longman.

—— (1973) *Consultation in Child Care*. Longman.

Fenichel, O. (1946) *The Psycho-Analytic Theory of Neurosis*. Kegan Paul.

Freud, A. (1946) *The Ego and the Mechanisms of Defence*. New York: International Universities Press.

Freud, S. (1910) *Leonardo da Vinci and a Memory of his Childhood*, in James Strachey, ed. *The Standard Edition of the Complete Psychological Works of Sigmund Freud*, 24 vols. Hogarth, 1953–73, vol. 11, pp. 63–137.

—— (1915) 'Instincts and their vicissitudes'. *S.E.* 14, pp. 117–40.

—— (1926) *Inhibitions, Symptoms and Anxiety*. *S.E.* 20, pp. 87–175.

Grolnick, S., ed. (1978) *Between Fantasy and Reality: Transitional Objects and Transitional Phenomena*. New York: Jason Aronson.

Laing, R. (1972) *Knots*. Harmondsworth: Penguin.

Langs, R. (1977) *The Therapeutic Interaction*. New York: Jason Aronson.

——— (1978) *The Listening Process.* New York: Jason Aronson.

Menzies Lyth, I. (1982) *The Psychological Welfare of Children Making Long Stays in Hospital: An Experience in the Art of the Possible.* Tavistock Institute of Human Relations Occasional Paper no. 3.

——— (1985) 'The development of the self in children in institutions', *J. Ch. Psychoth.* 2(2).

——— (1989) 'Day care of children under five', in *The Dynamics of the Social: Selected Essays.* Free Association Books.

Poincaré, H. (1908) 'Mathematical creation', in *The Foundations of Science,* G.B. Halstead, trans. Science Press, 1924.

Redl, F. (1966) *When We Deal with Children.* New York: Free Press.

Sechehaye, M. (1951) *Symbolic Realization.* New York: International Universities Press (Monograph Series on Schizophrenia).

Tod, R., ed. (1968) *Disturbed Children.* Longman.

Winnicott, D. (1958) *Collected Papers. Through Paediatrics to Psycho-Analysis.* Tavistock.

——— (1965) 'The mentally ill in your caseload', in *The Maturational Processes and the Facilitating Environment.* Hogarth, 1972, pp. 217–29.

——— (1986) *Home is Where We Start From.* Harmondsworth: Penguin.

Index